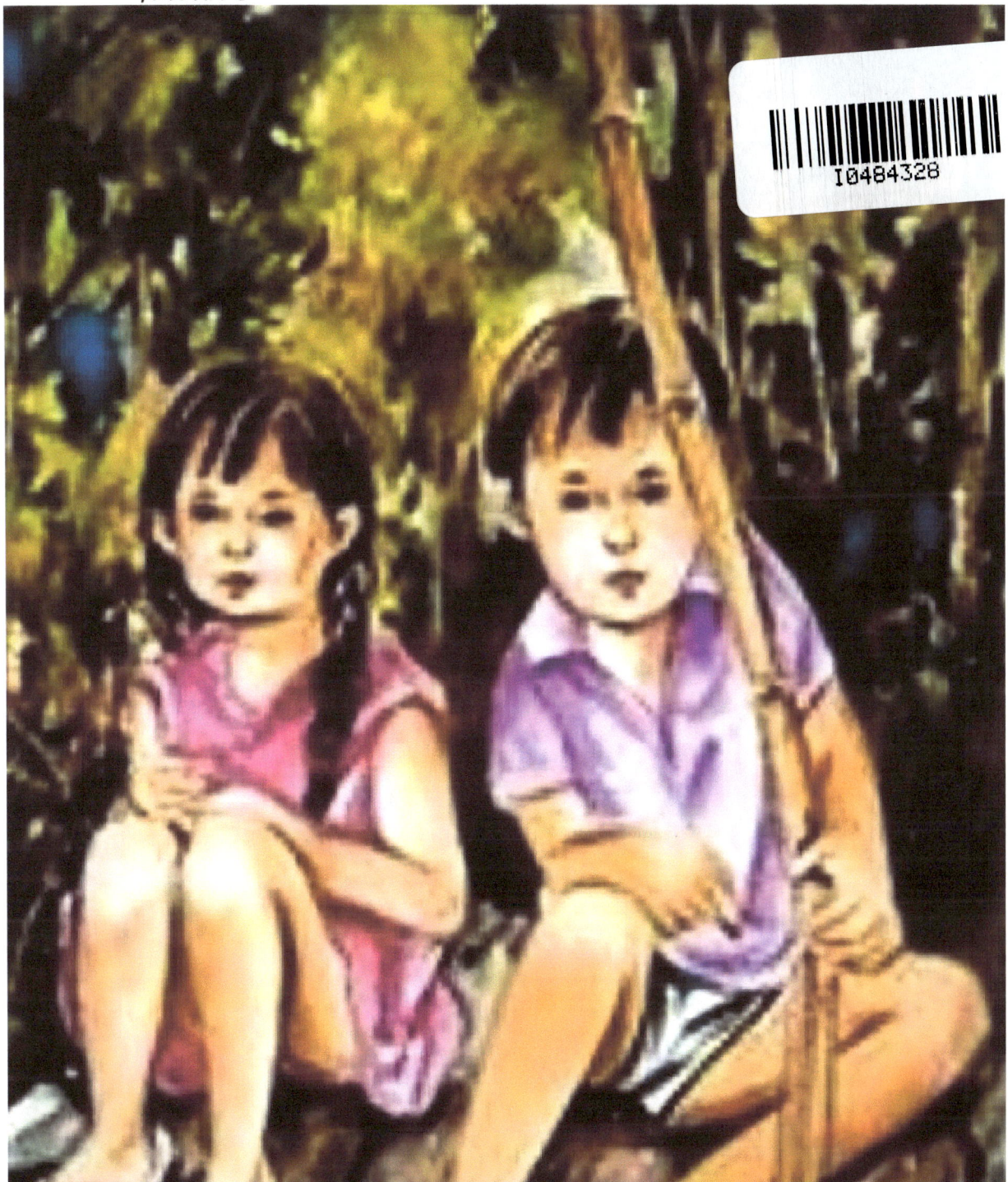

Siblings, by Joeyboi Galang. His paintings or commissioned works available on request.

WELCOME! We hope you enjoy this Fave Art-8 collection of my favorite art works. Most art works are copied from the internet, posters, pictures and books. They are computer-generated and enhanced digitally. You may display this book as coffee table book in your living room, as conversation piece. You may give this as gift . You may cut out and frame each page. Each art work is 8.5x11 inches and suitable for framing, and then wall decors. Most art works are done by me, the self-publisher, via computer enhancement. Some paintings are courtesy of my friends, such as Joeyboi Galang and Jomel Lugtu. You can order paintings from them or ask them to do commission works. Just contact their facebook accounts. Or contact me.

The ISBN Code Numbers of this book are:
ISBN-13: 978- 1503000551 & ISBN-10: 1503000559
Printed in USA. Free to copy by anybody. Why copy? Just buy the book.
My other books list can be accessed at:
http://tinyurl.com/mj76ccq and http://www.jobelizes.webs.com.
My contact email is job_elizes@yahoo.com. (Tatay Jobo Elizes, Pub.)

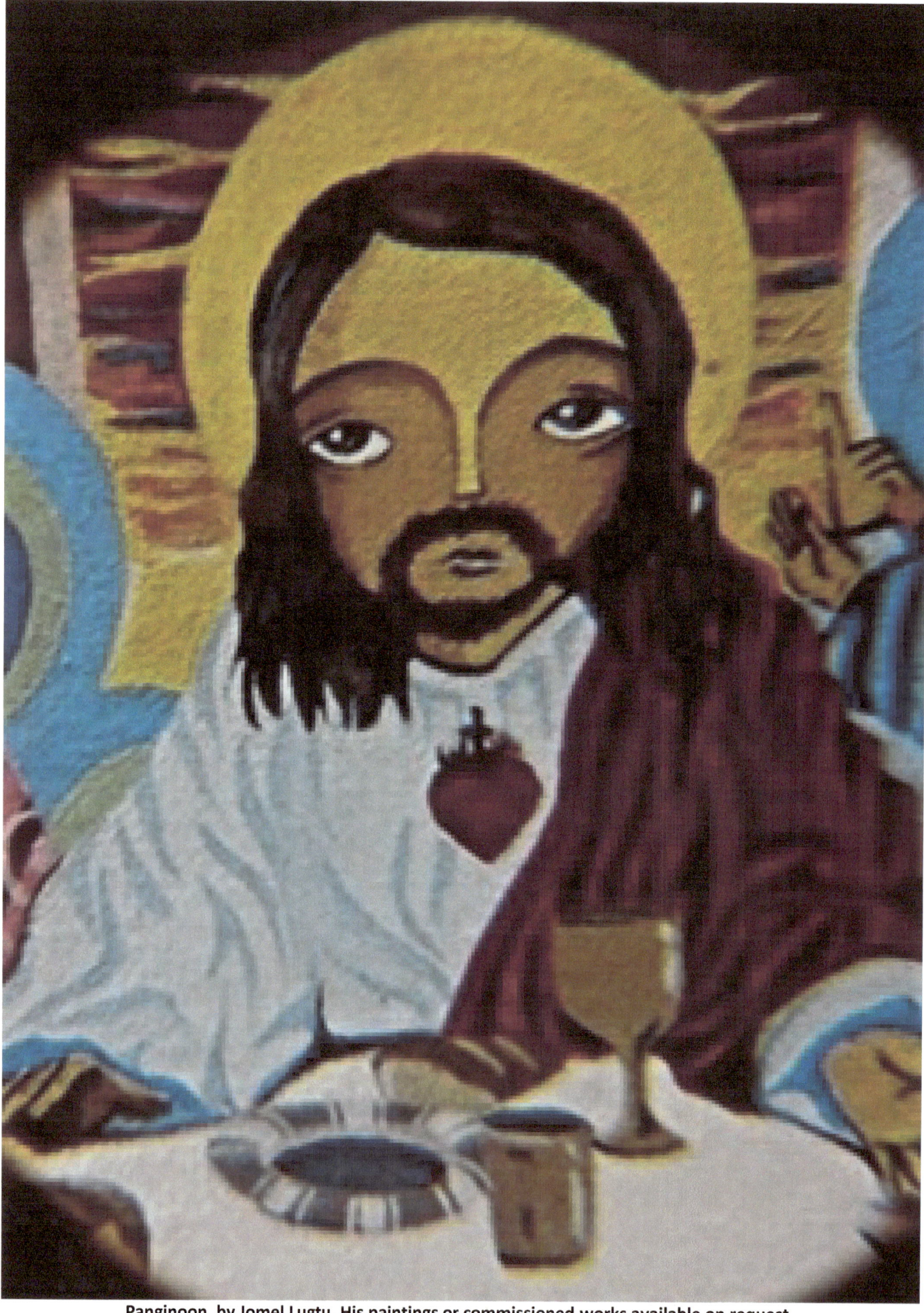

Panginoon, by Jomel Lugtu. His paintings or commissioned works available on request.

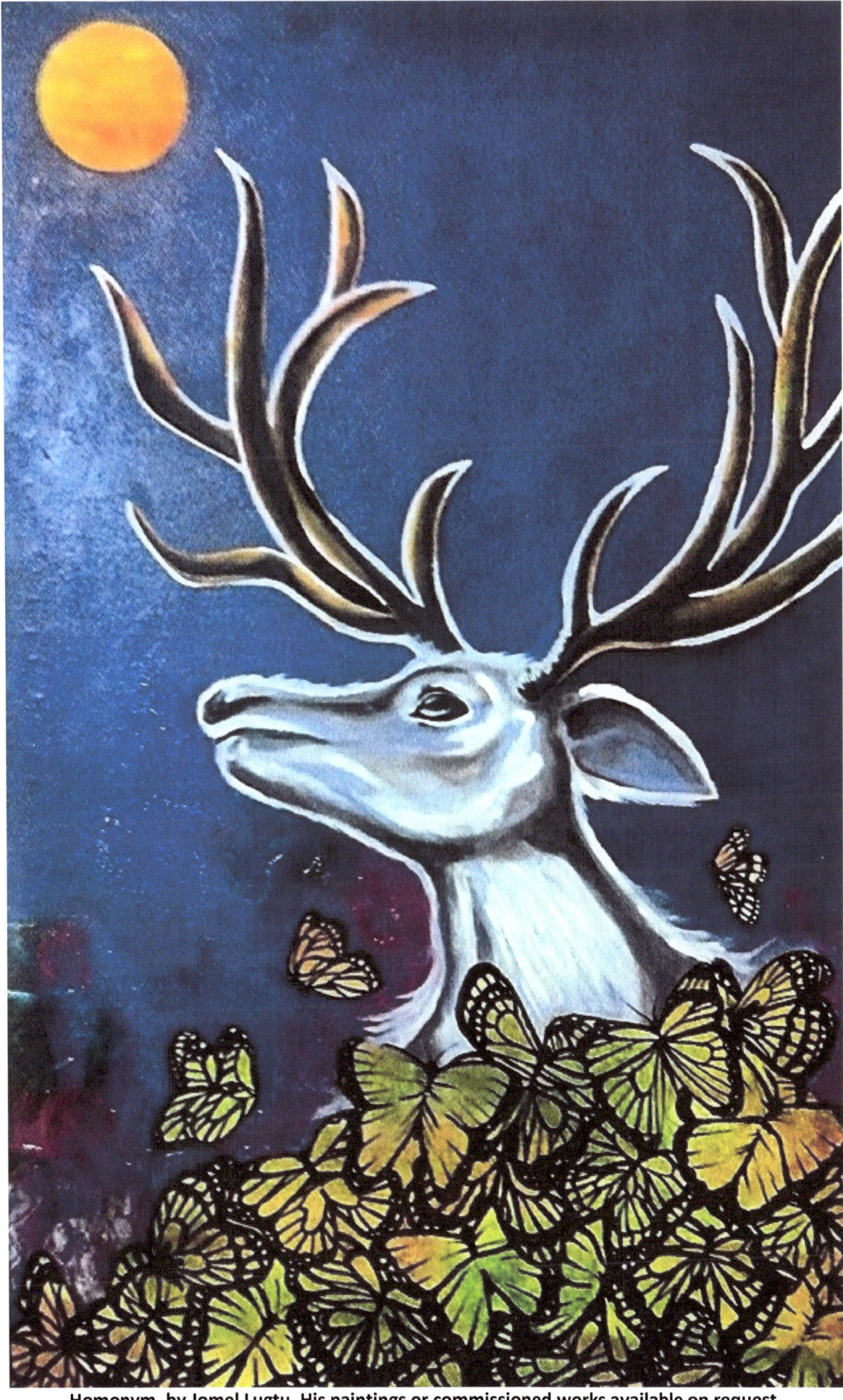

Homonym, by Jomel Lugtu. His paintings or commissioned works available on request.

The Last Supper, by Jomel Lugtu. His paintings or commissioned works available on request.

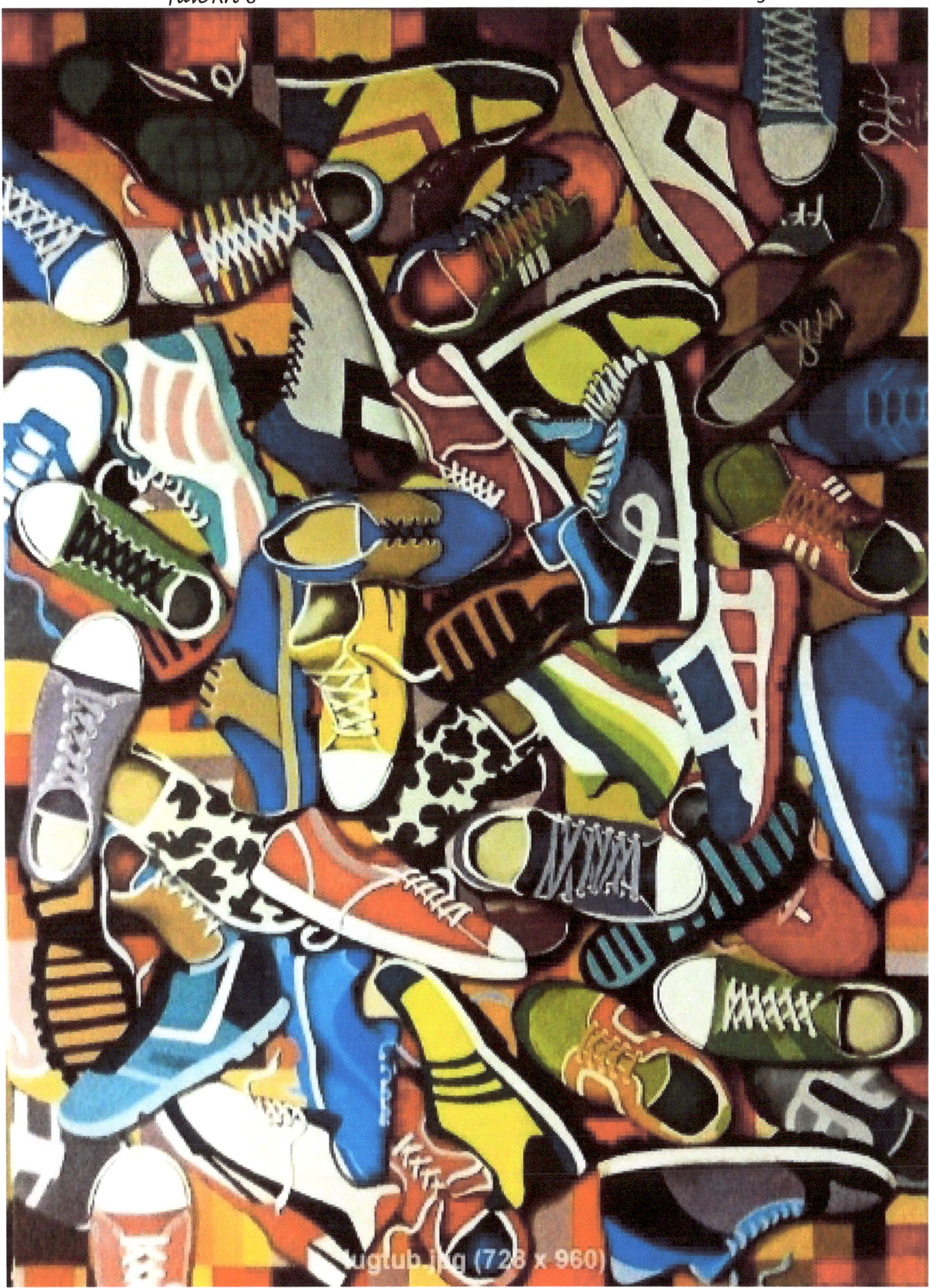

Shoes, by Jomel Lugtu. His paintings or commissioned works available on request.

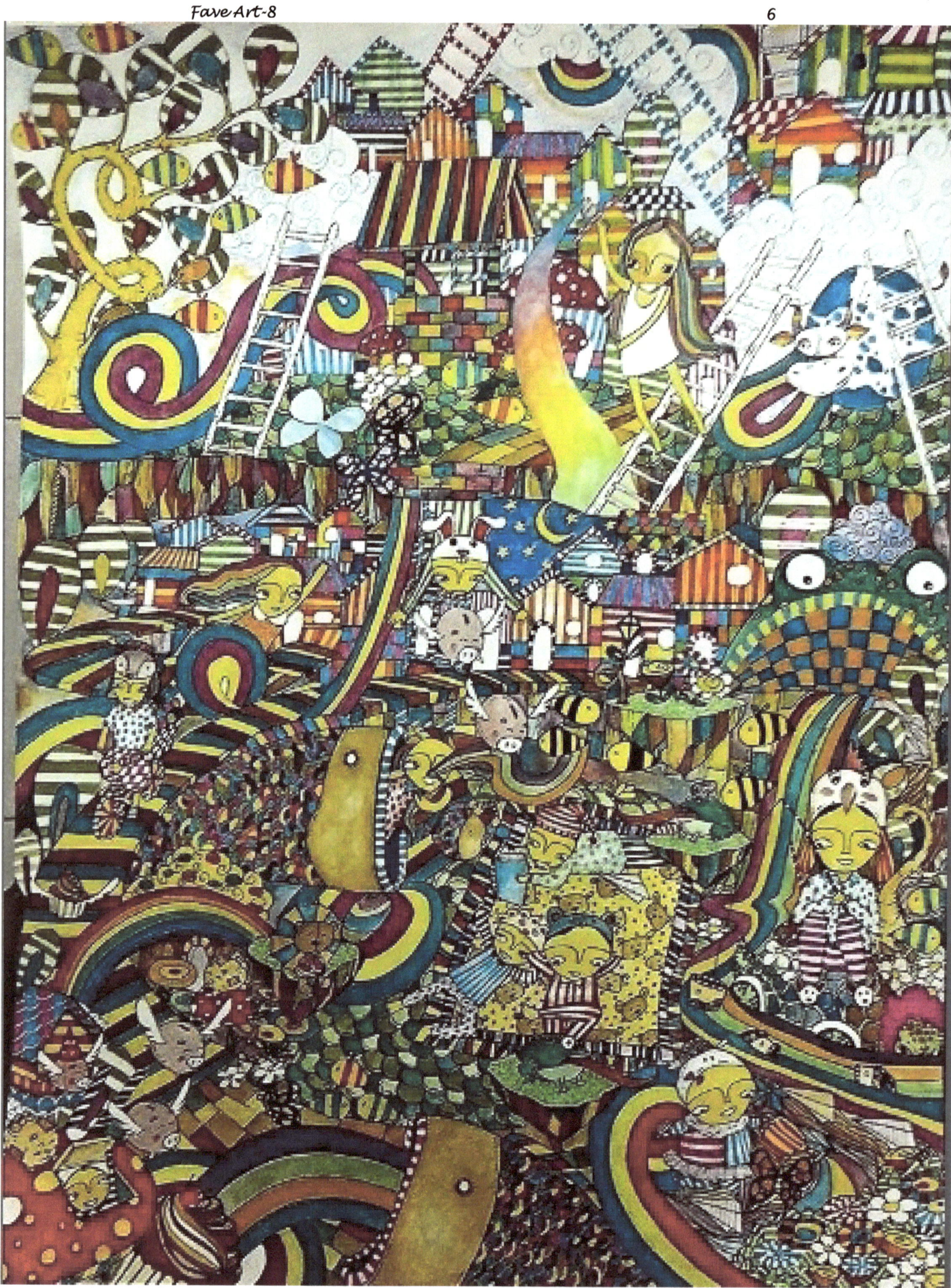

The Underland, Dream Series, by Jomel Lugtu. His paintings or commissioned works available on request.

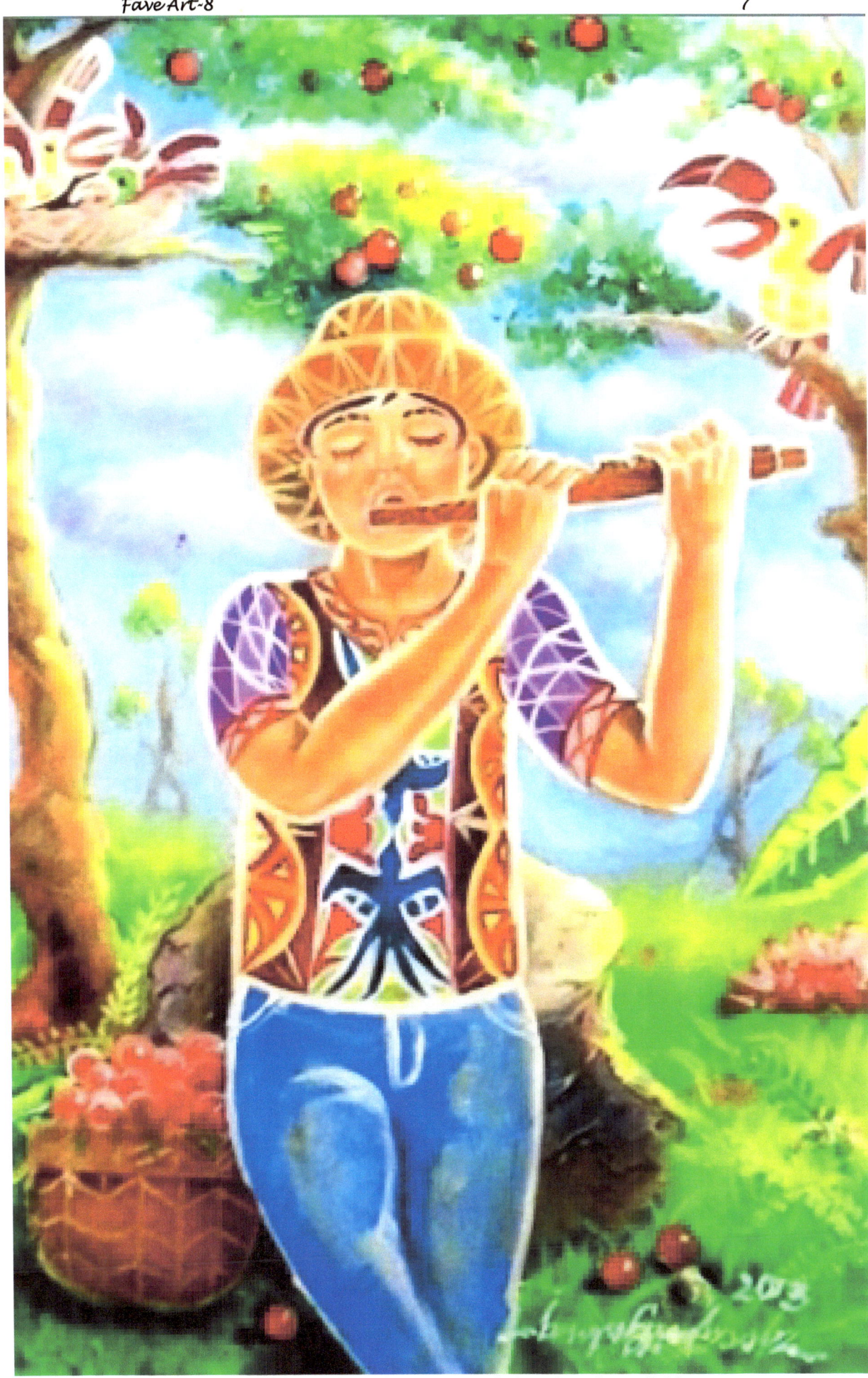

Flutist, by Joeyboi Galang. His paintings or commissioned works available on request.

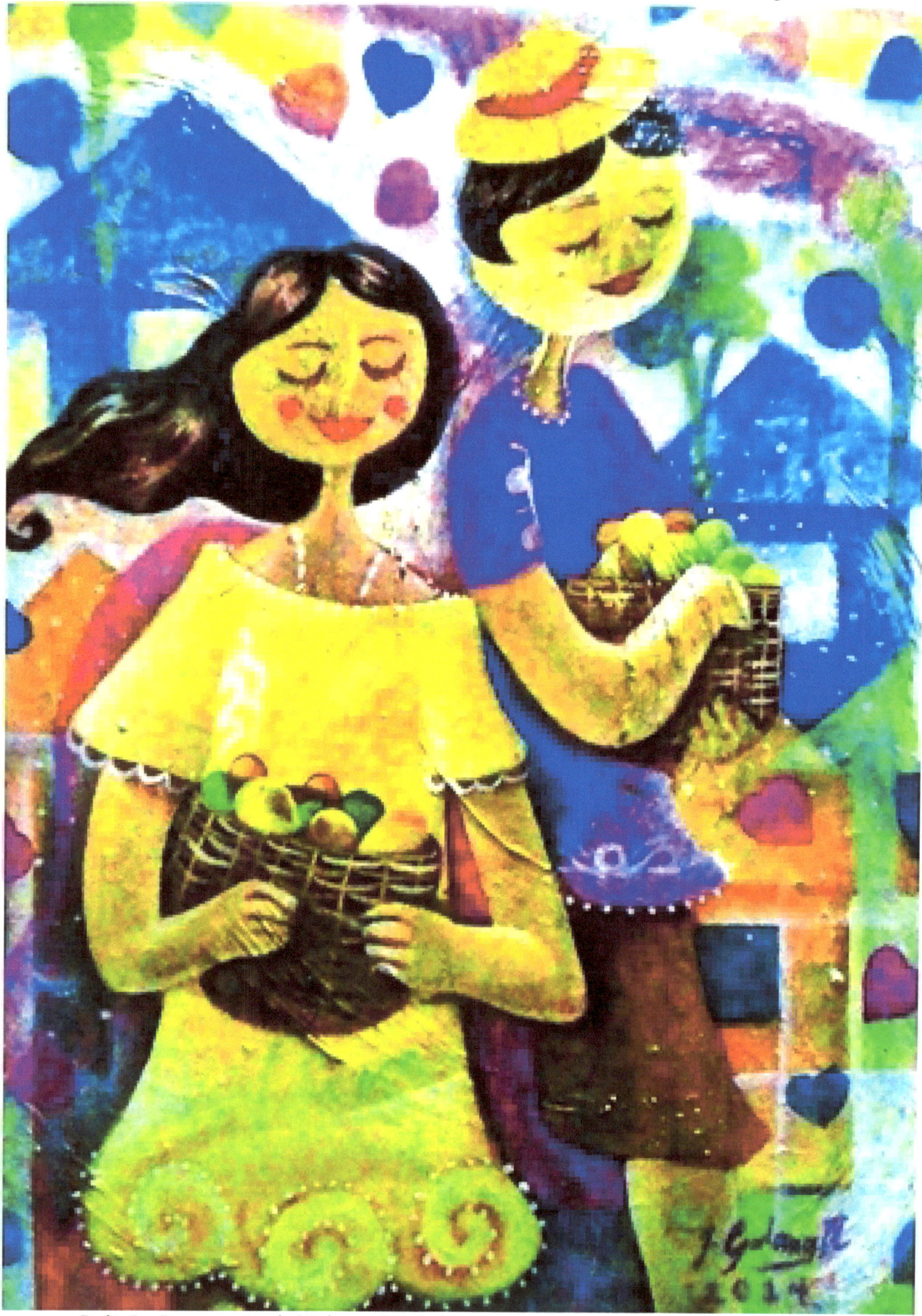

Fruits For Everyone, Joyeboi Galang. His paintings or commissioned works available on request.

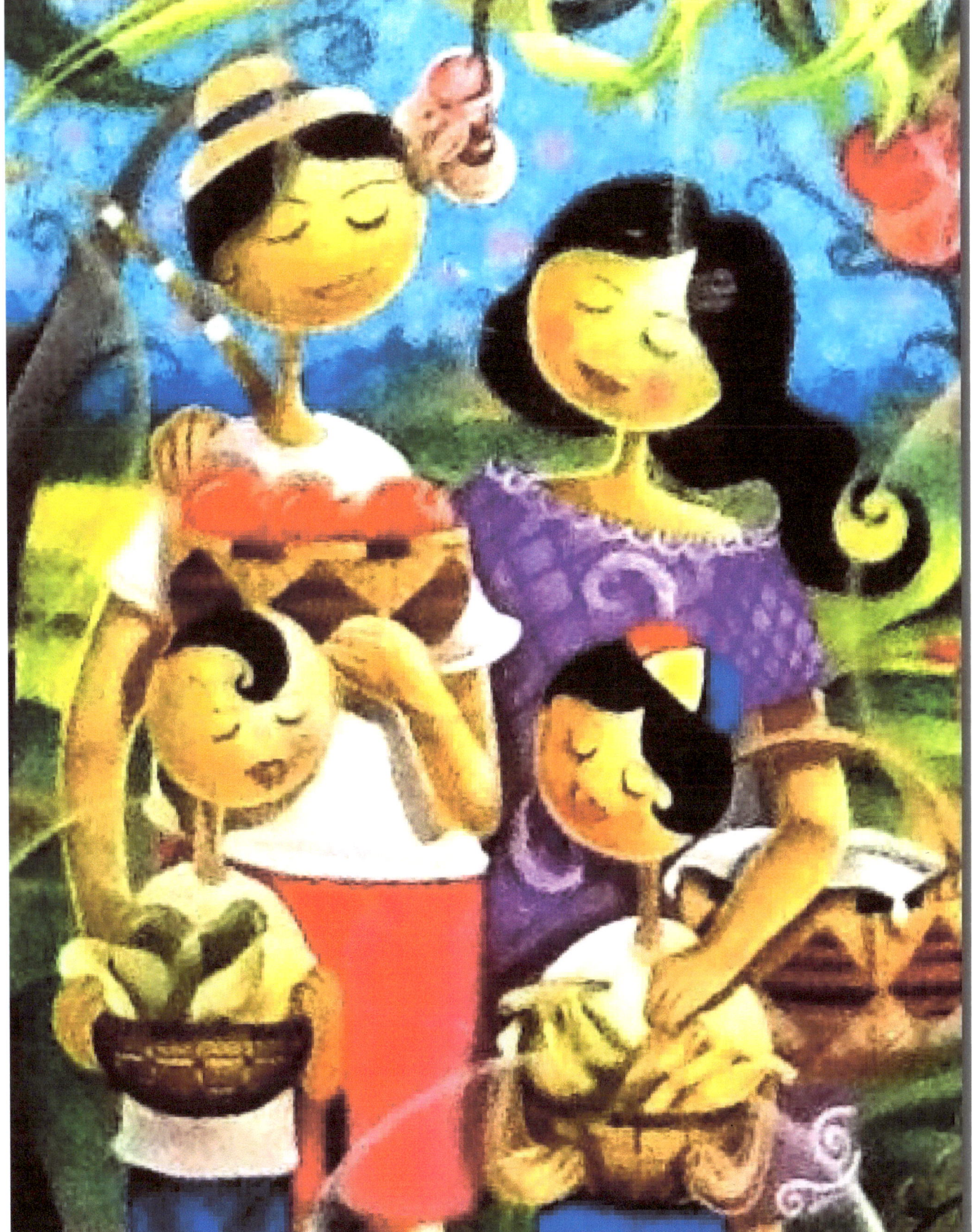

Fruit Lovers, by Joeyboi Galang. His paintings or commissioned works available on request.

WELCOME! We hope you enjoy this Fave Art-8 collection of my favorite art works. Most art works are copied from the internet, posters, pictures and books. They are computer-generated and enhanced digitally. You may display this book as coffee table book in your living room, as conversation piece. You may give this as gift. You may cut out and frame each page. Each art work is 8.5x11 inches and suitable for framing.

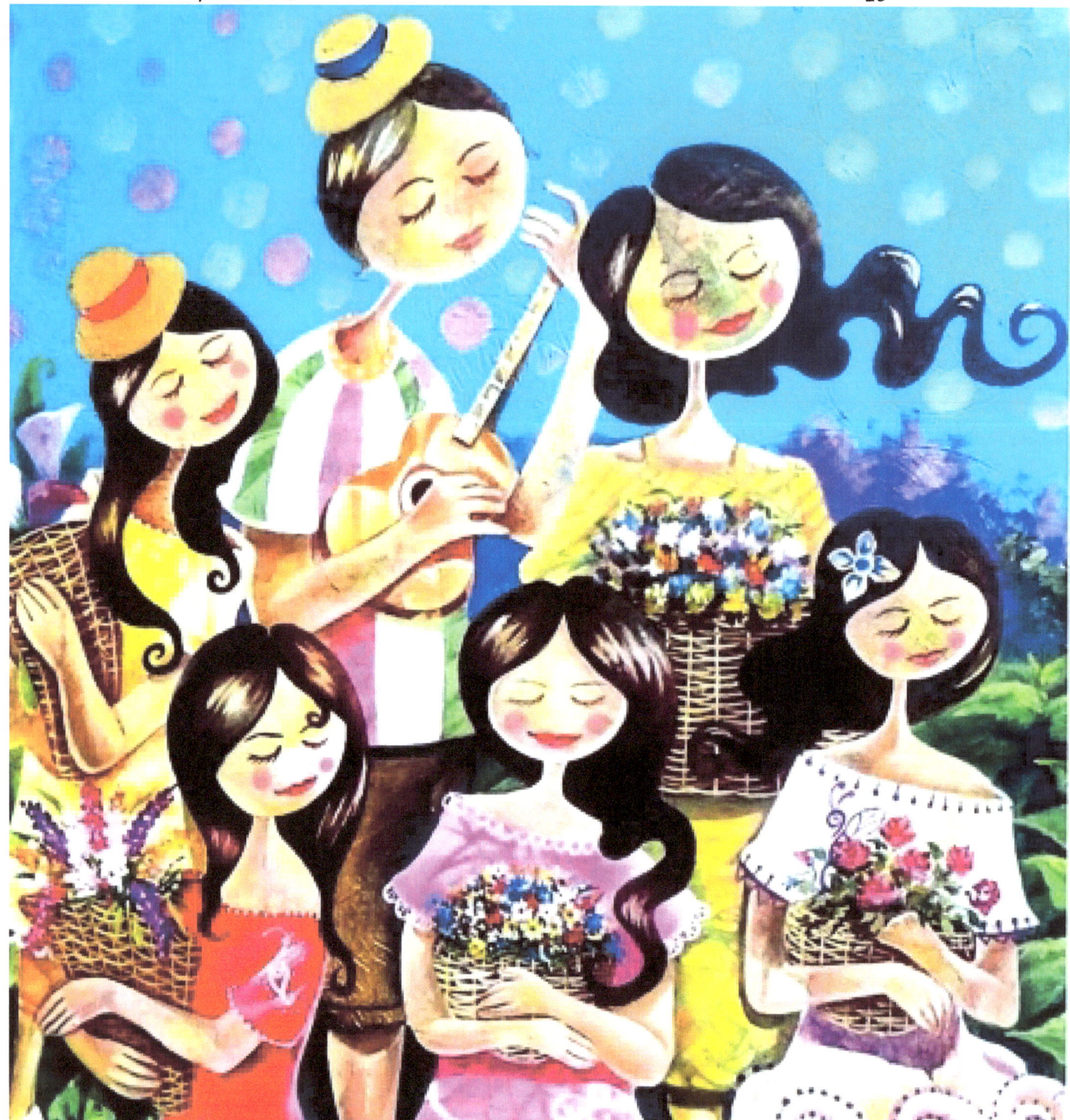

Family Bound By Love, by Joeyboi Galang. His paintings or commissioned works available on request.

WELCOME! We hope you enjoy this Fave Art-8 collection of my favorite art works. Most art works are copied from the internet, posters, pictures and books. They are computer-generated and enhanced digitally. You may display this book as coffee table book in your living room, as conversation piece. You may give this as gift . You may cut out and frame each page. Each art work is 8.5x11 inches and suitable for framing, and then wall decors. Most art works are done by me, the self-publisher, via computer enhancement.

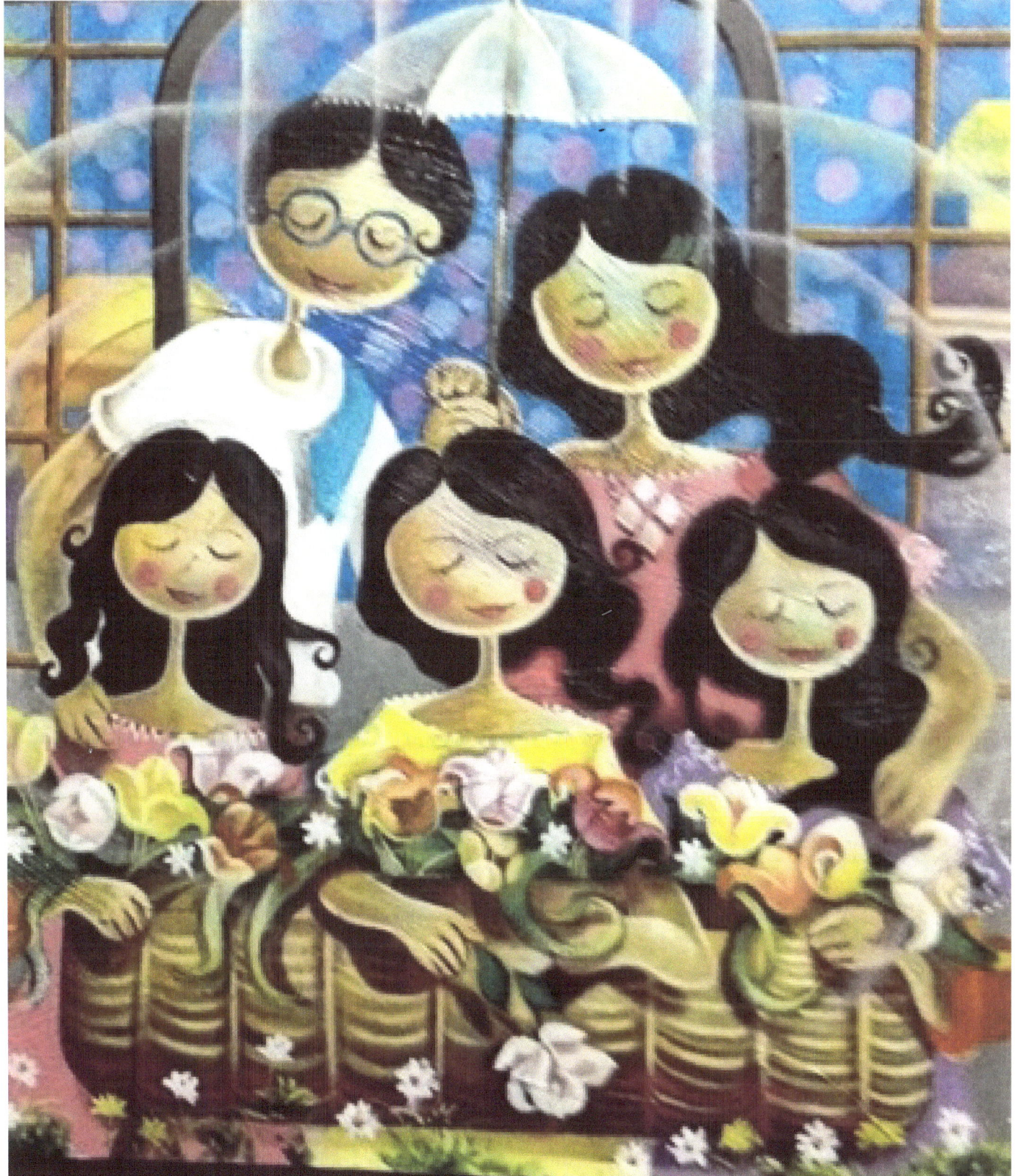

Girls with Flower Baskets, by Joeyboi Galang. His paintings or commissioned works available on request.

WELCOME! We hope you enjoy this Fave Art-8 collection of my favorite art works. Most art works are copied from the internet, posters, pictures and books. They are computer-generated and enhanced digitally. You may display this book as coffee table book in your living room, as conversation piece. You may give this as gift . You may cut out and frame each page. Each art work is 8.5x11 inches and suitable for framing, and then wall decors. Most art works are done by me, the self-publisher, via computer enhancement.

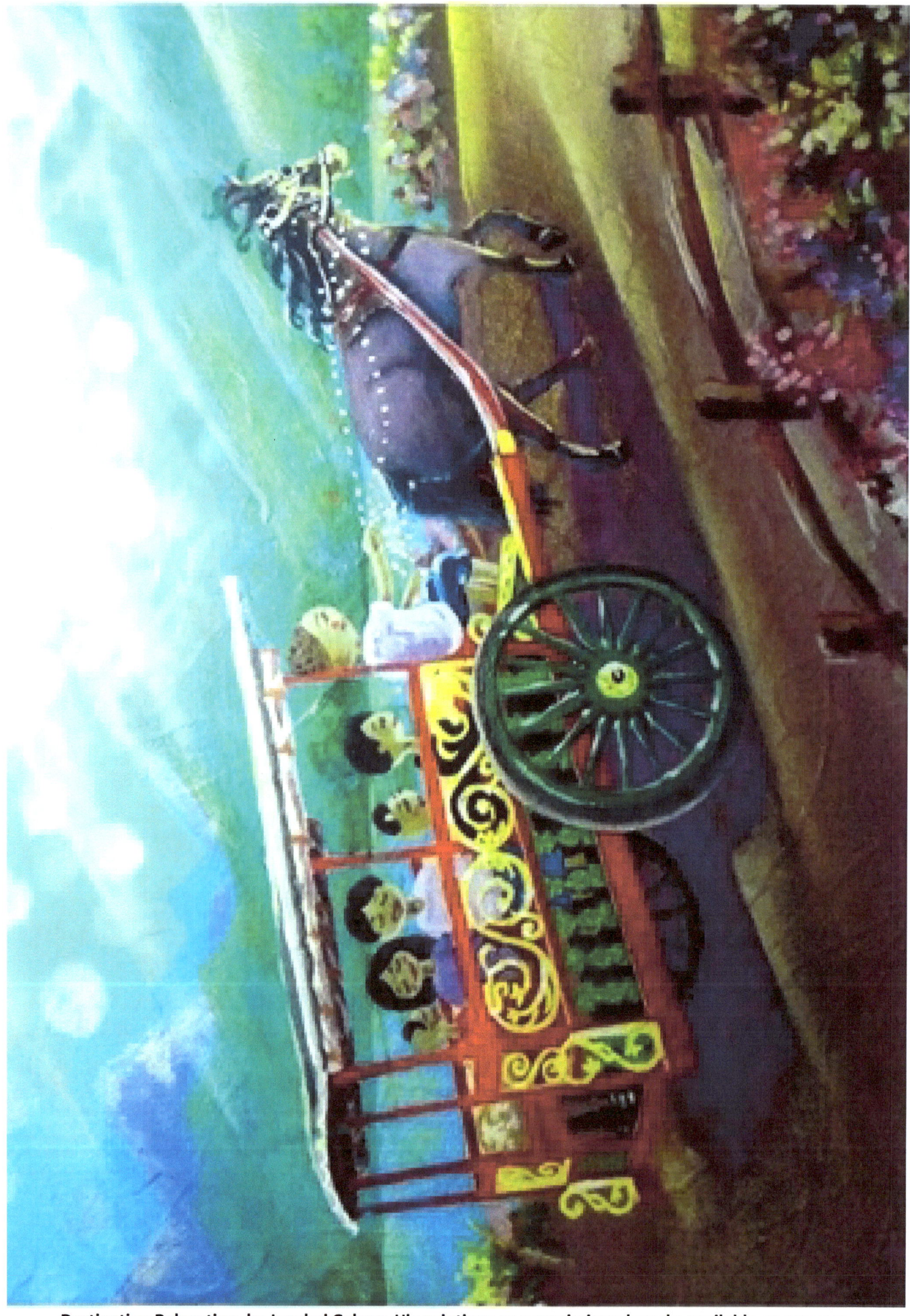

Destination Relaxation, by Joeyboi Galang. His paintings or commissioned works available on request.

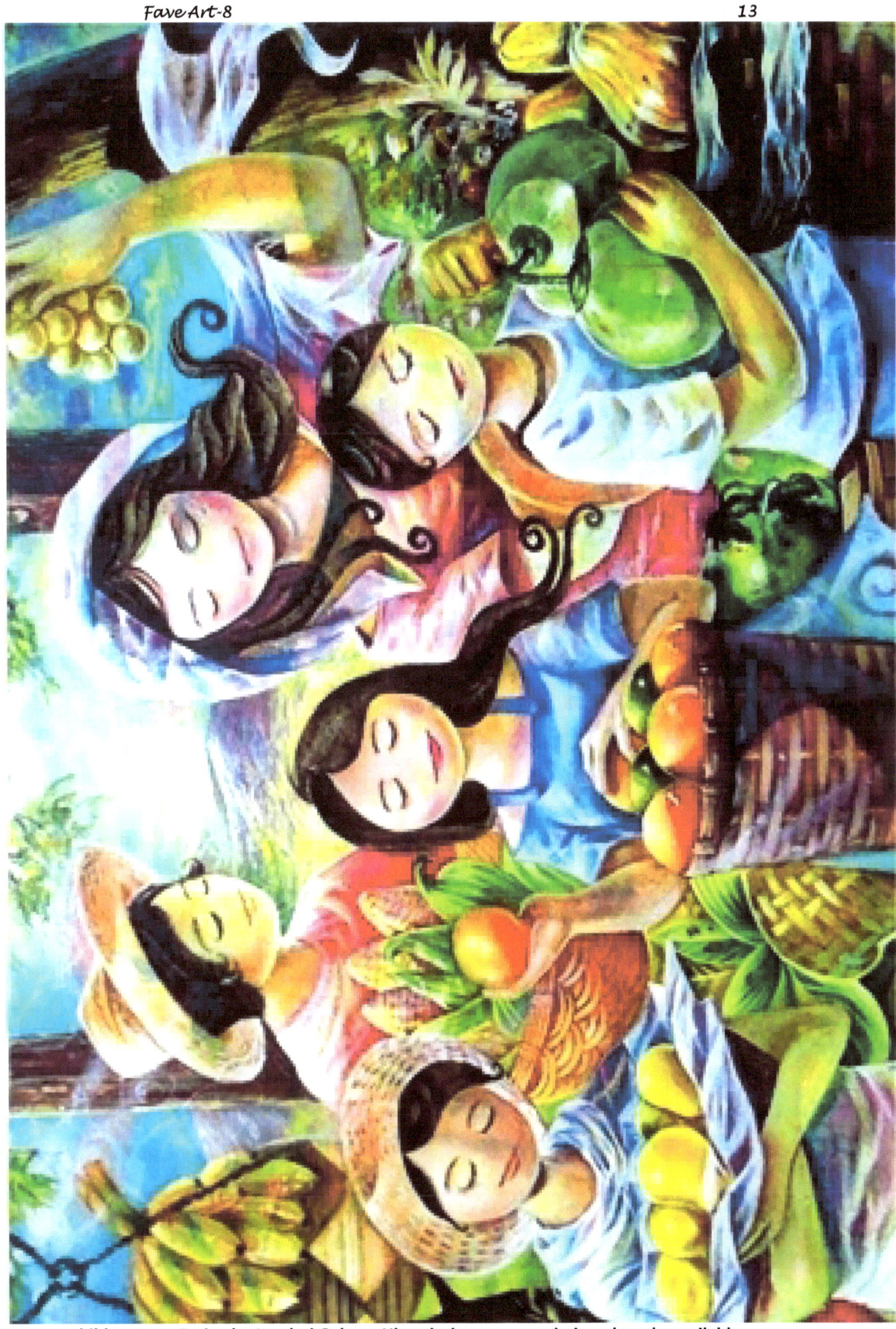

Children Love Fruits, by Joeyboi Galang. His paintings or commissioned works available on request.

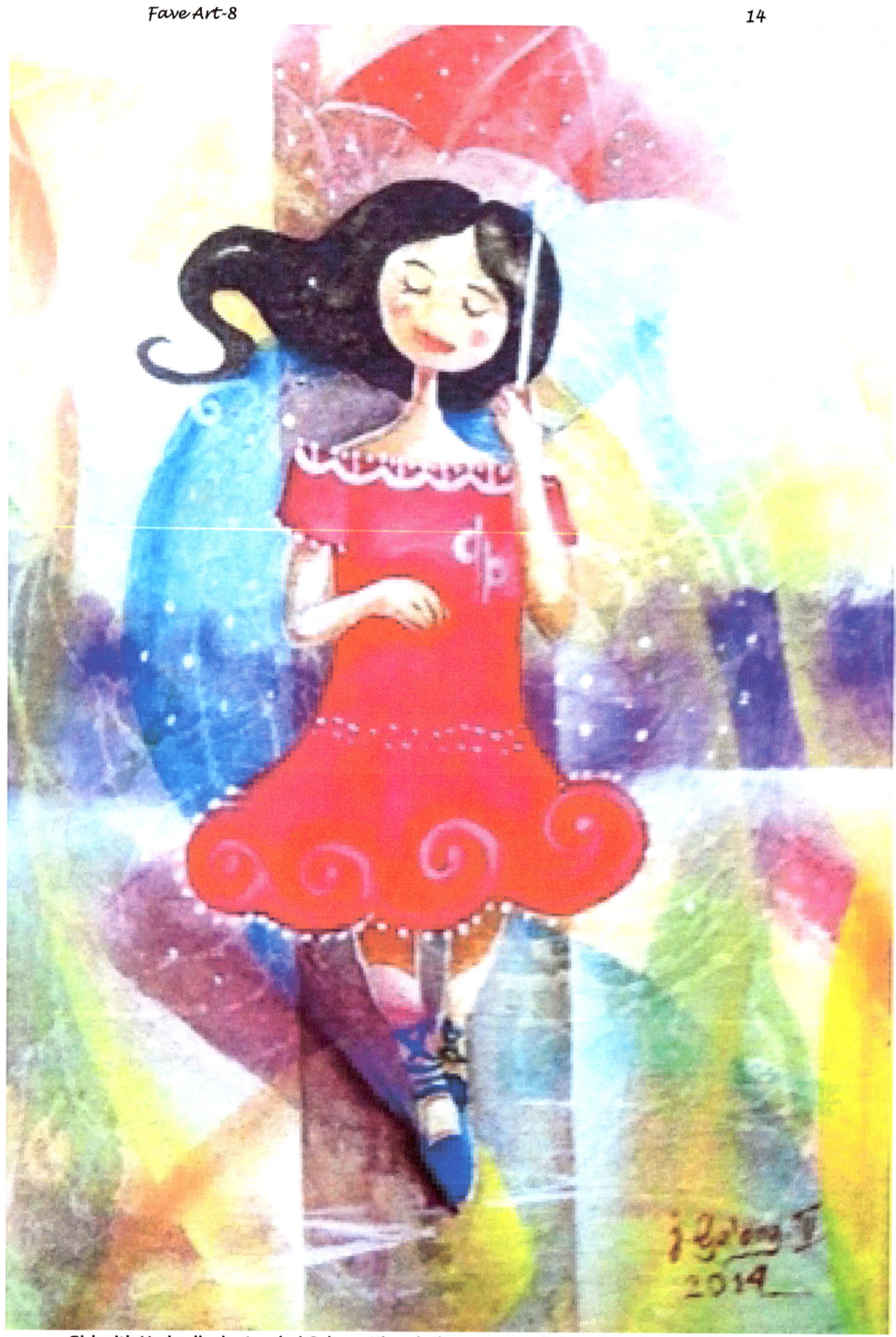

Girl with Umbrella, by Joeyboi Galang. His paintings or commissioned works available on request.

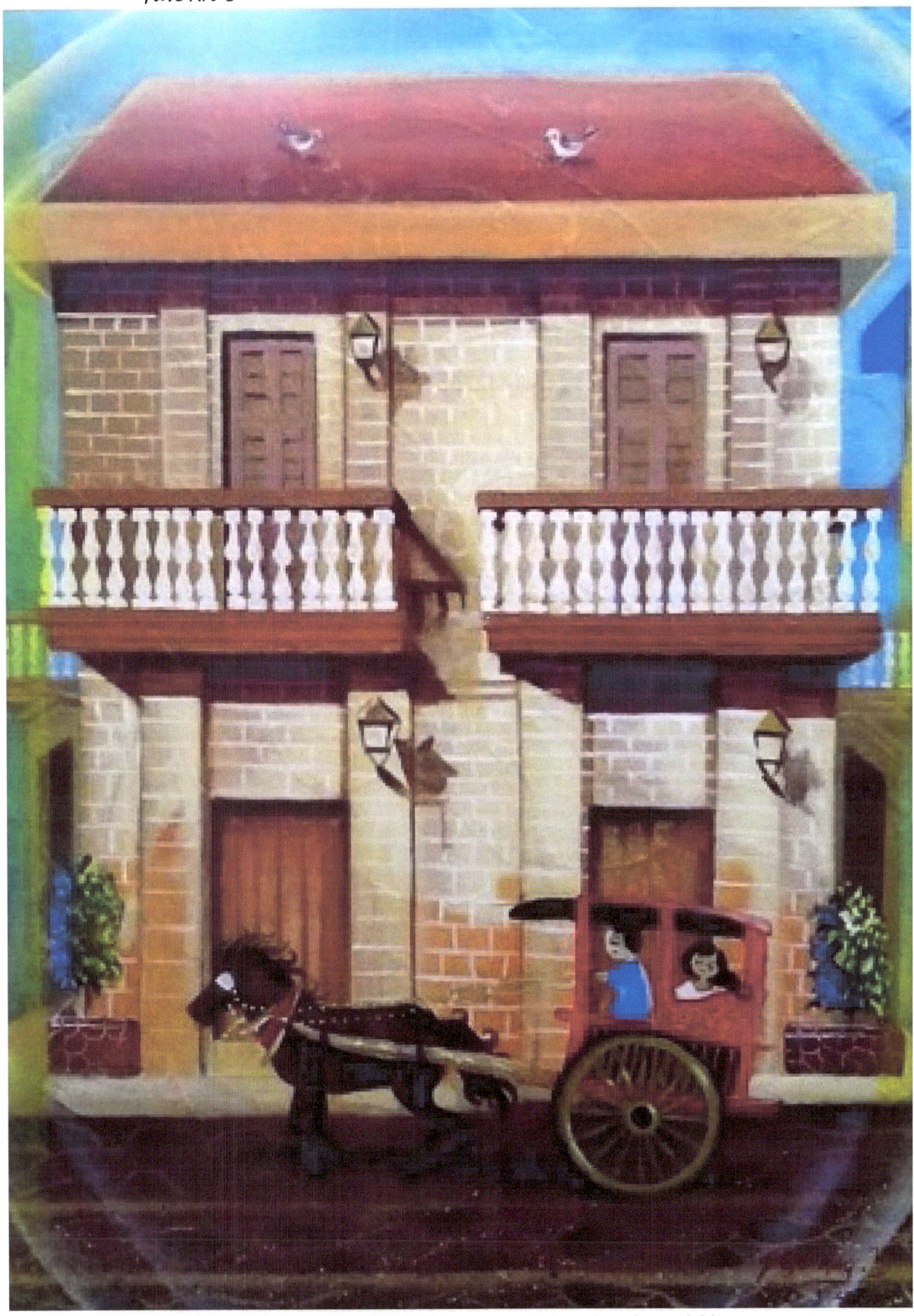

Happy Ride, by Joeyboi Galang. His paintings or commissioned works available on request.

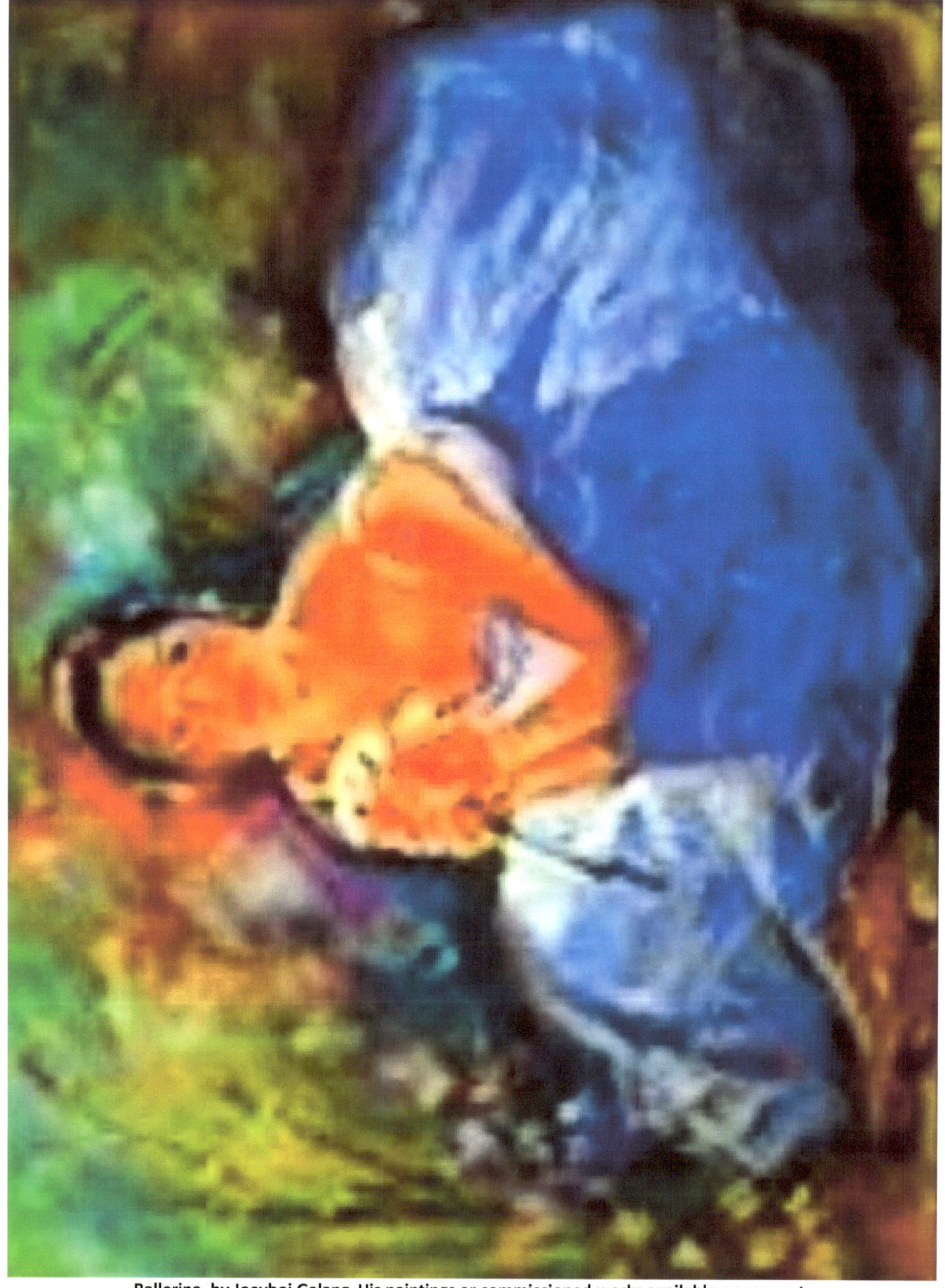

Ballerina, by Joeyboi Galang. His paintings or commissioned works available on request.

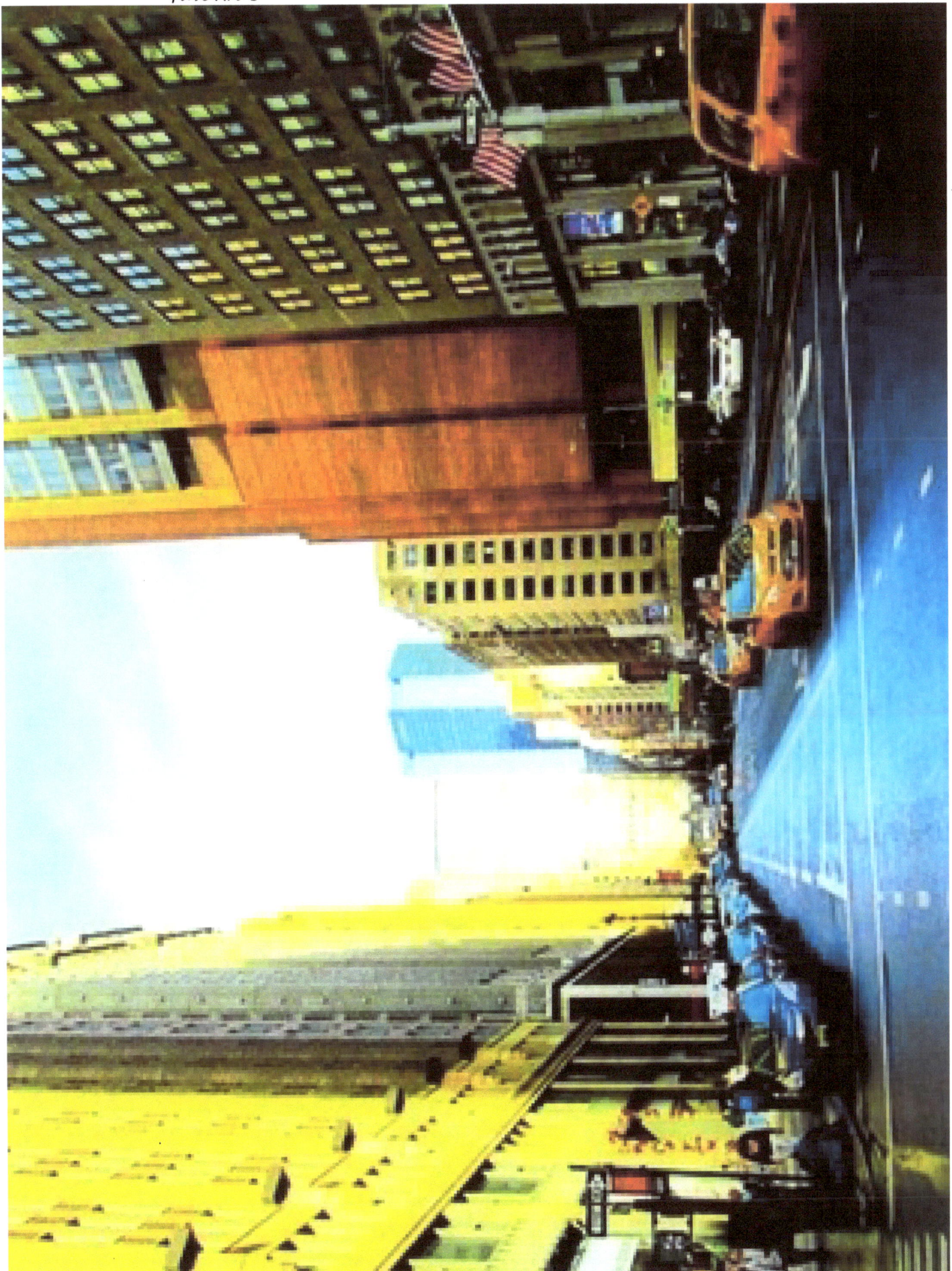

Typical Manhattan Street in NYC

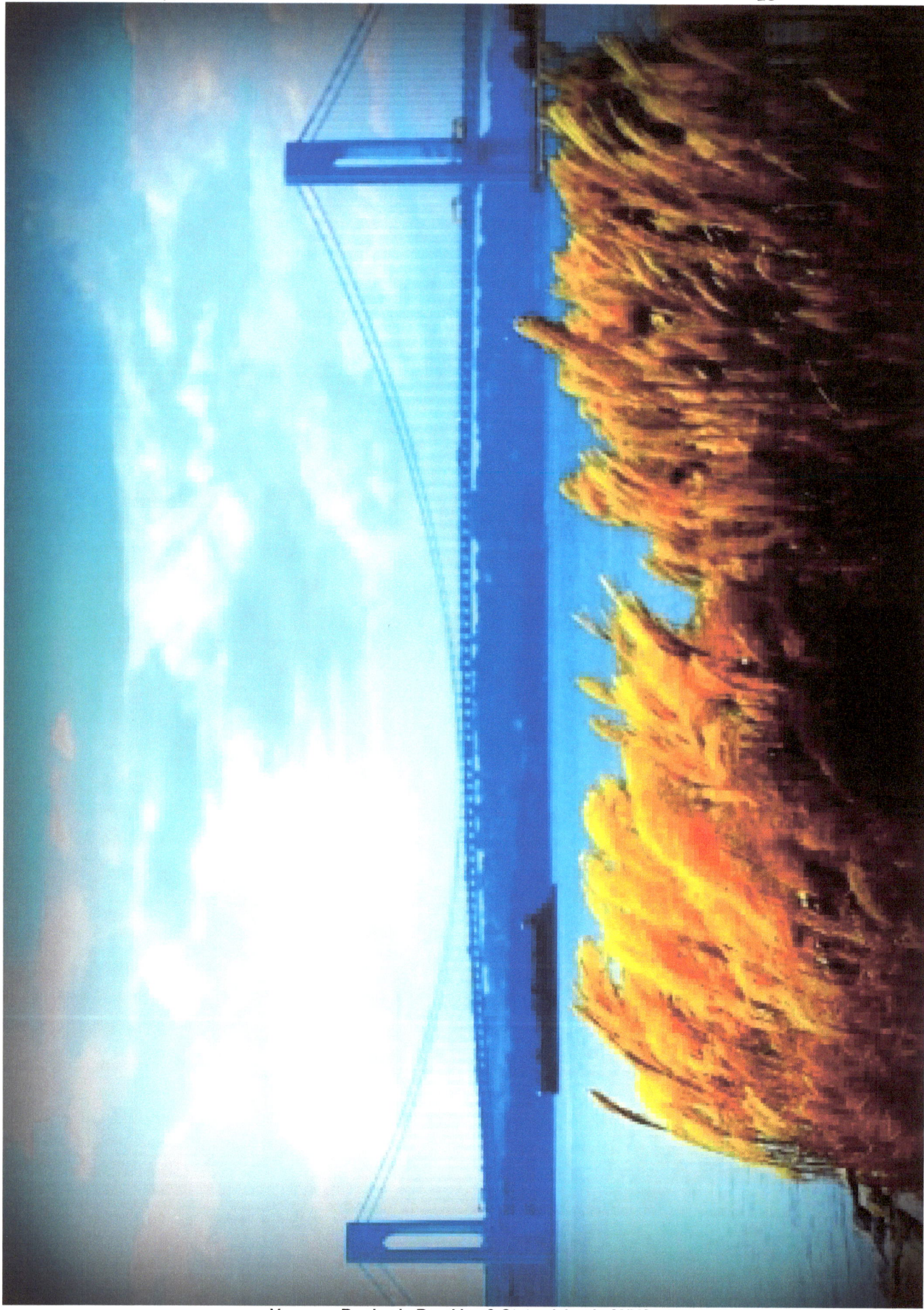

Verazano Brudge in Brooklyn & Staten Island of NYC

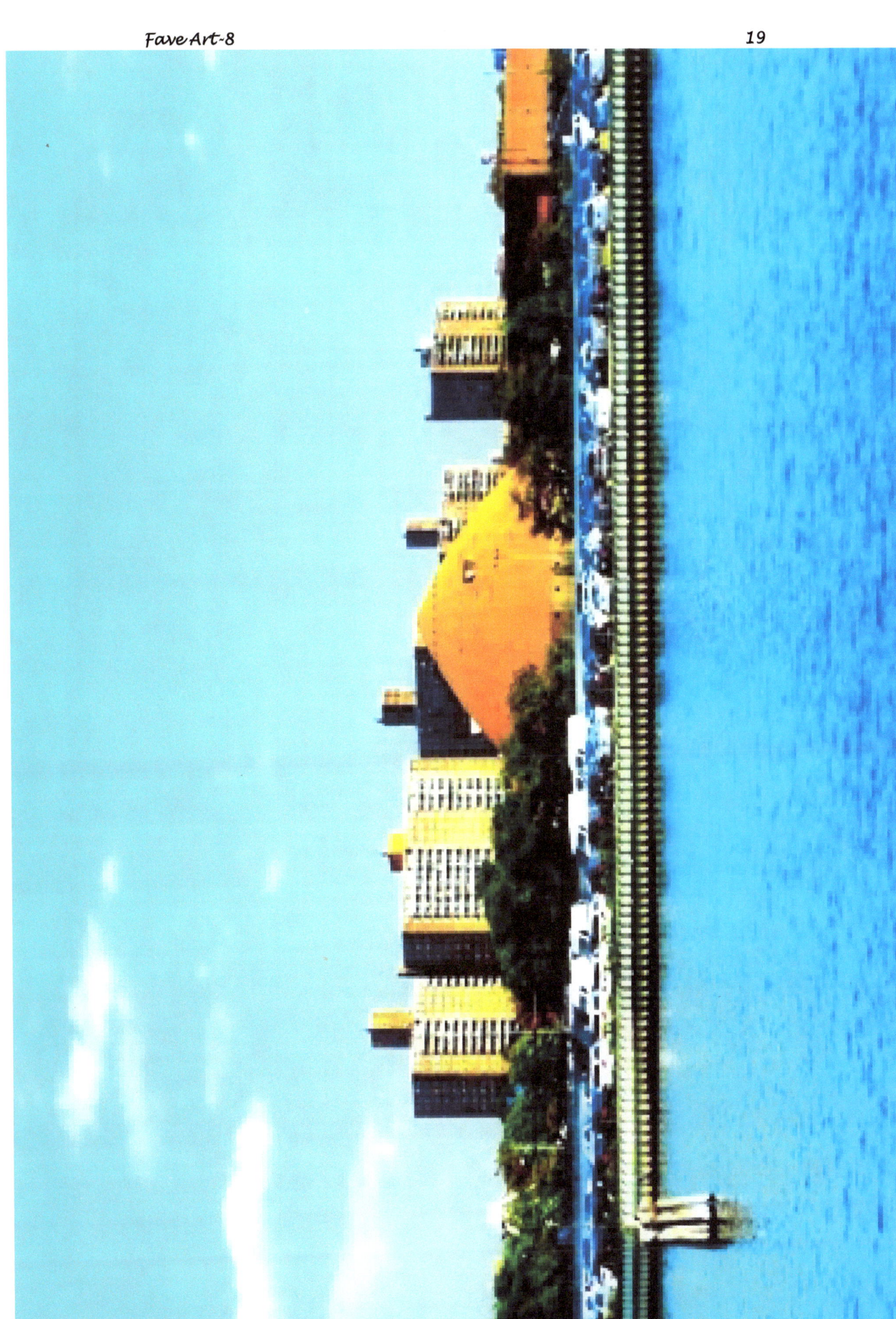

My Brooklyn neighborhood near marine side in NYC

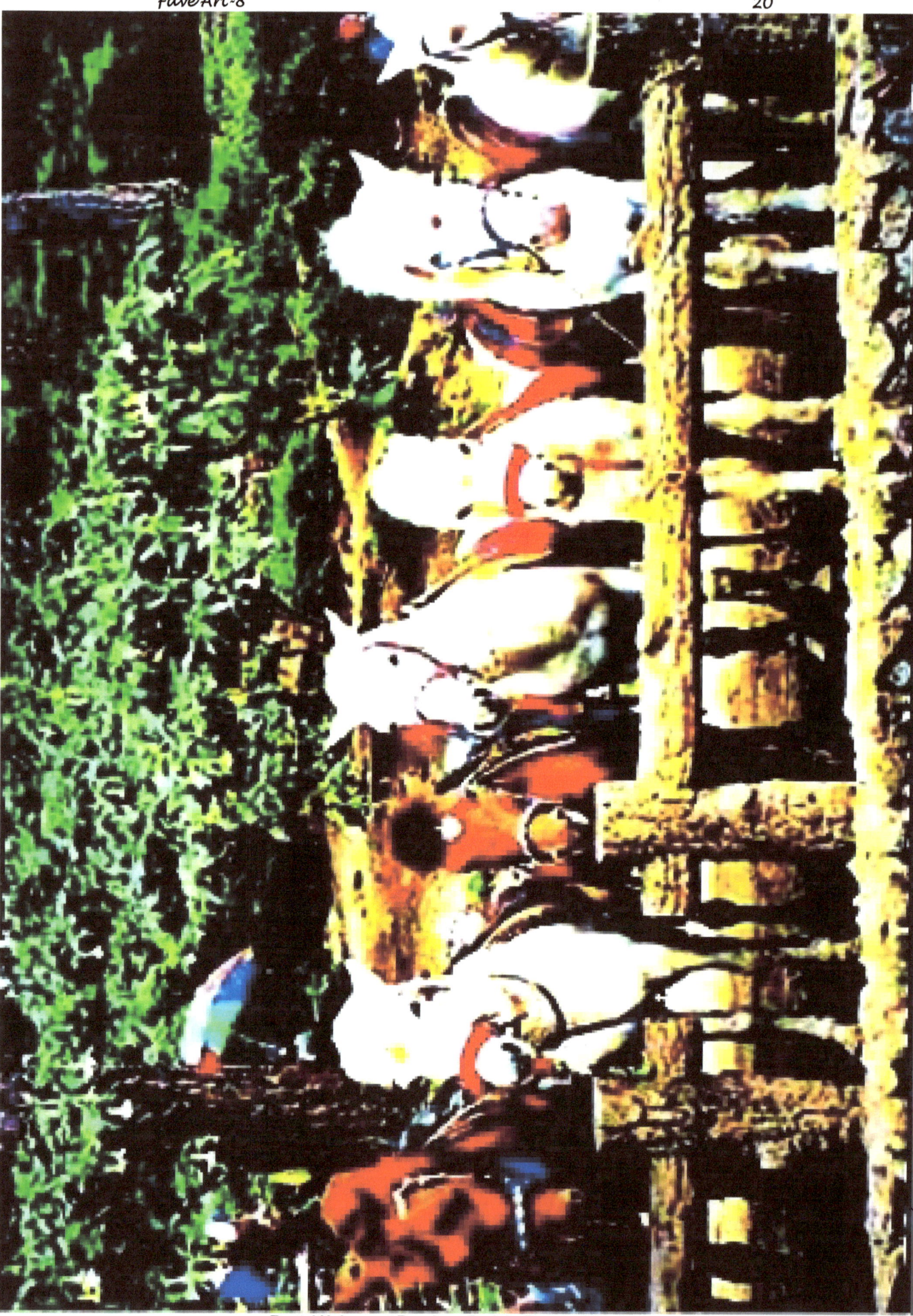

Rental Hoirses at Burnham Park in Baguio City, Phl

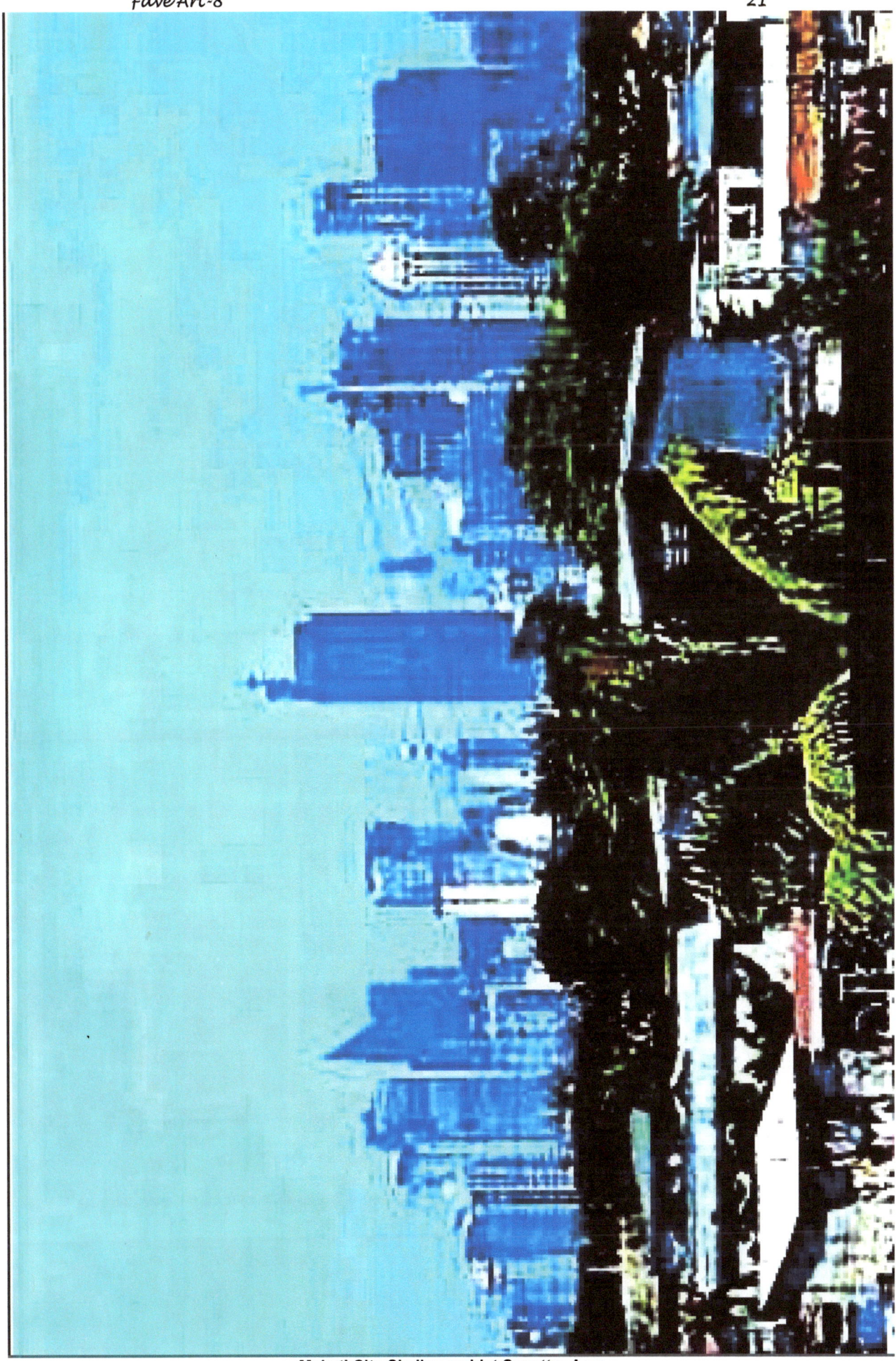

Makati City Skyline amidst Squatter Area

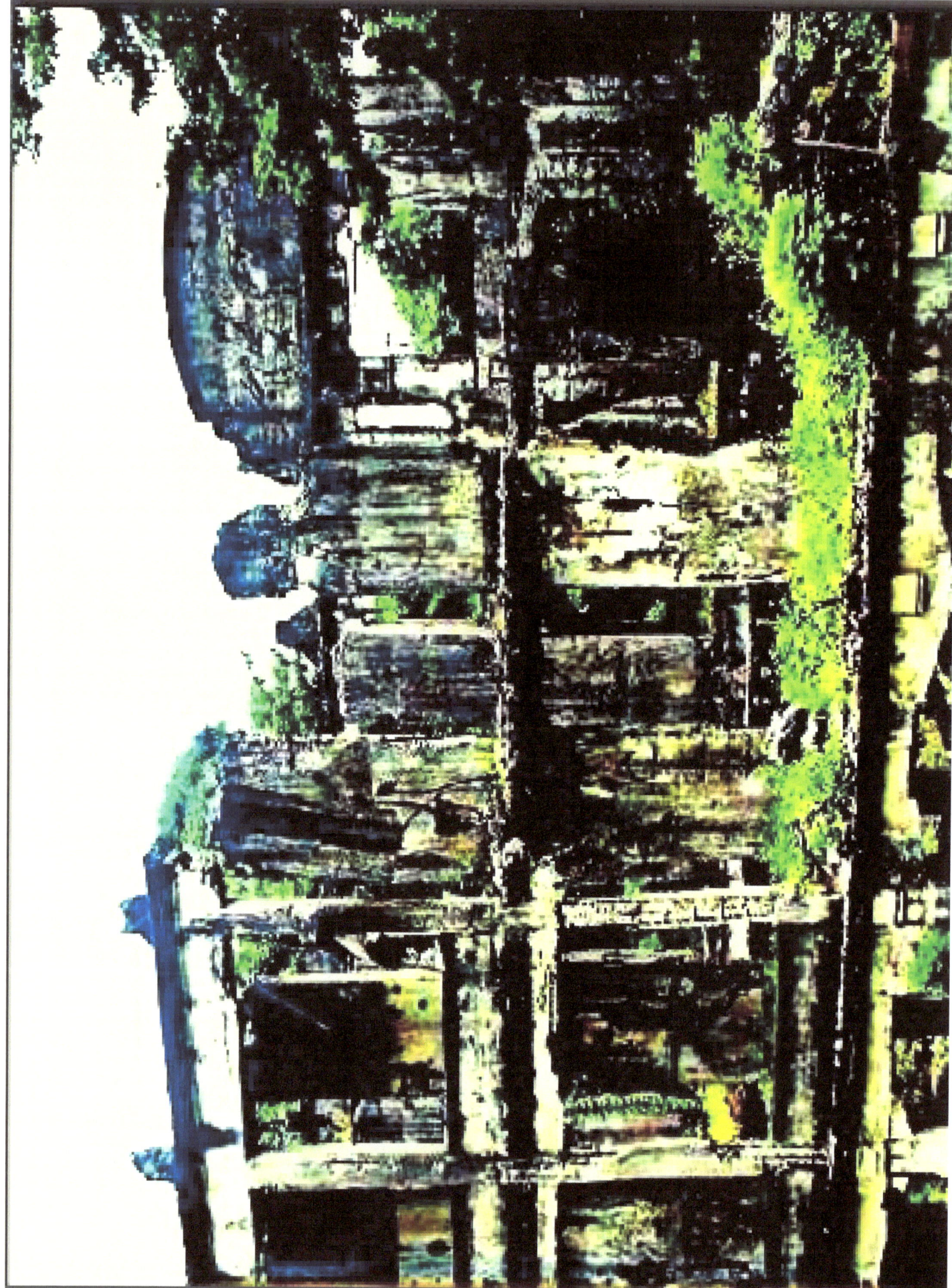

Corregidor Ruins, Phl

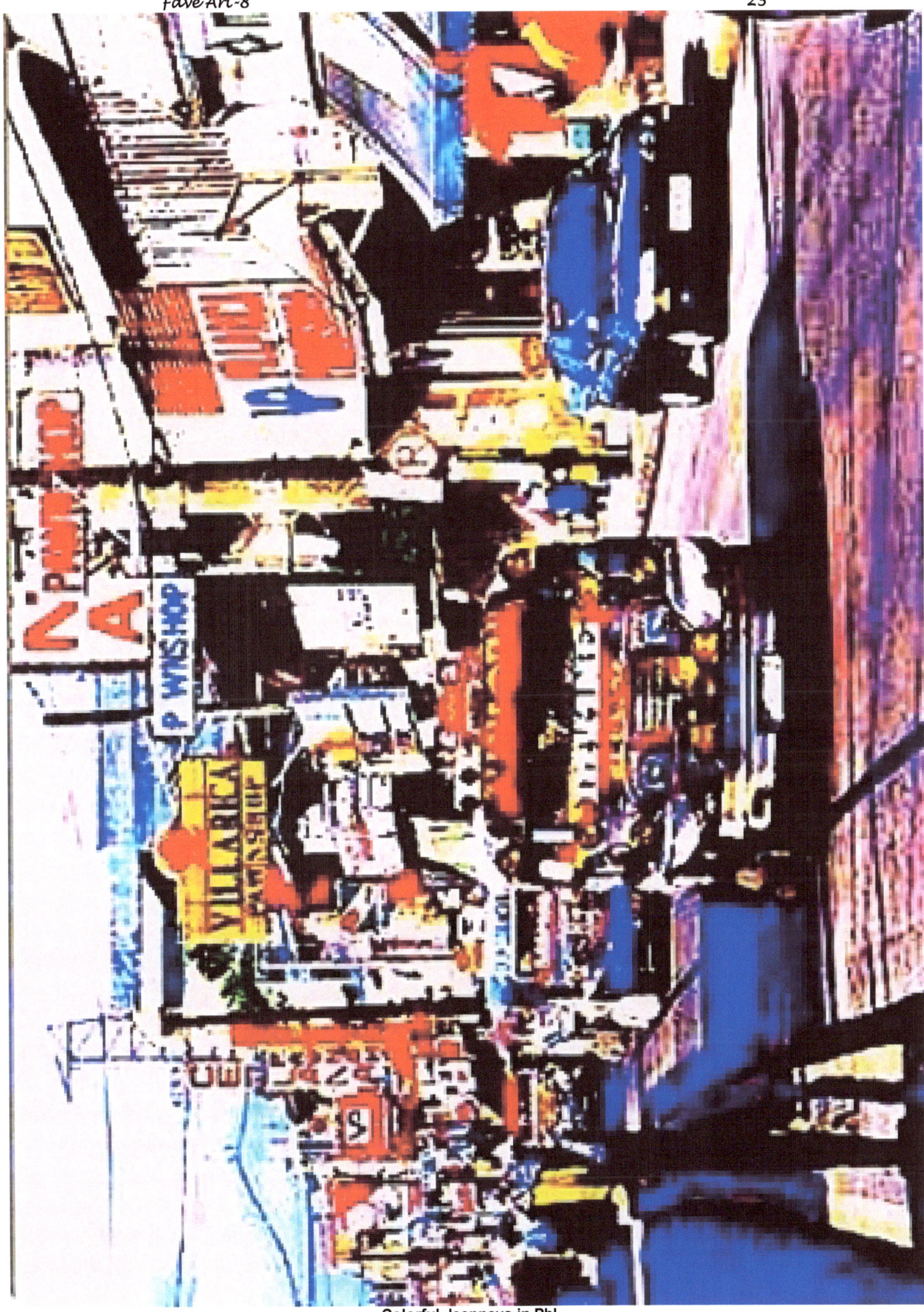

Colorful Jeepneys in Phl

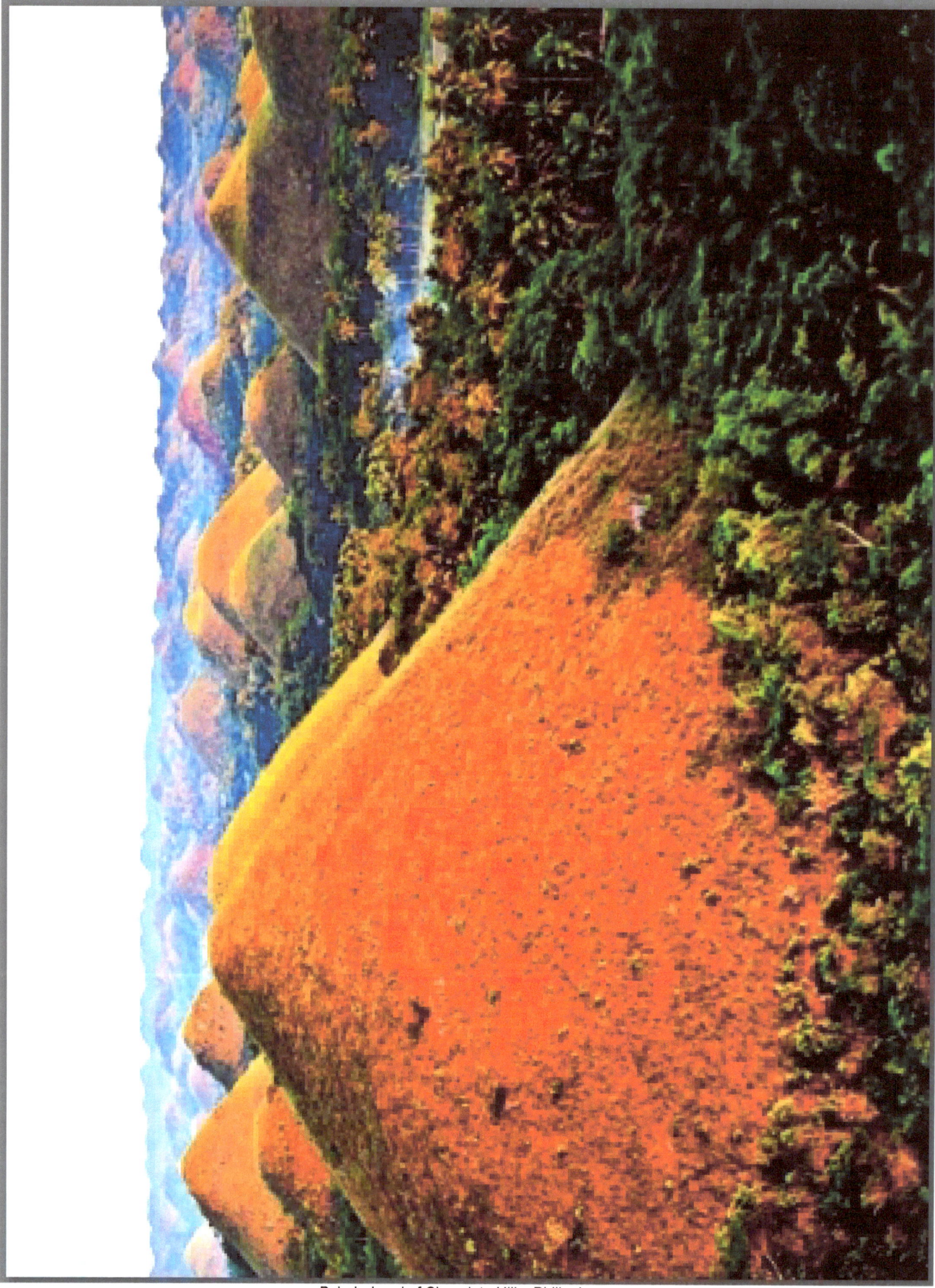

Bohol - Land of Chocolate Hills, Philippines

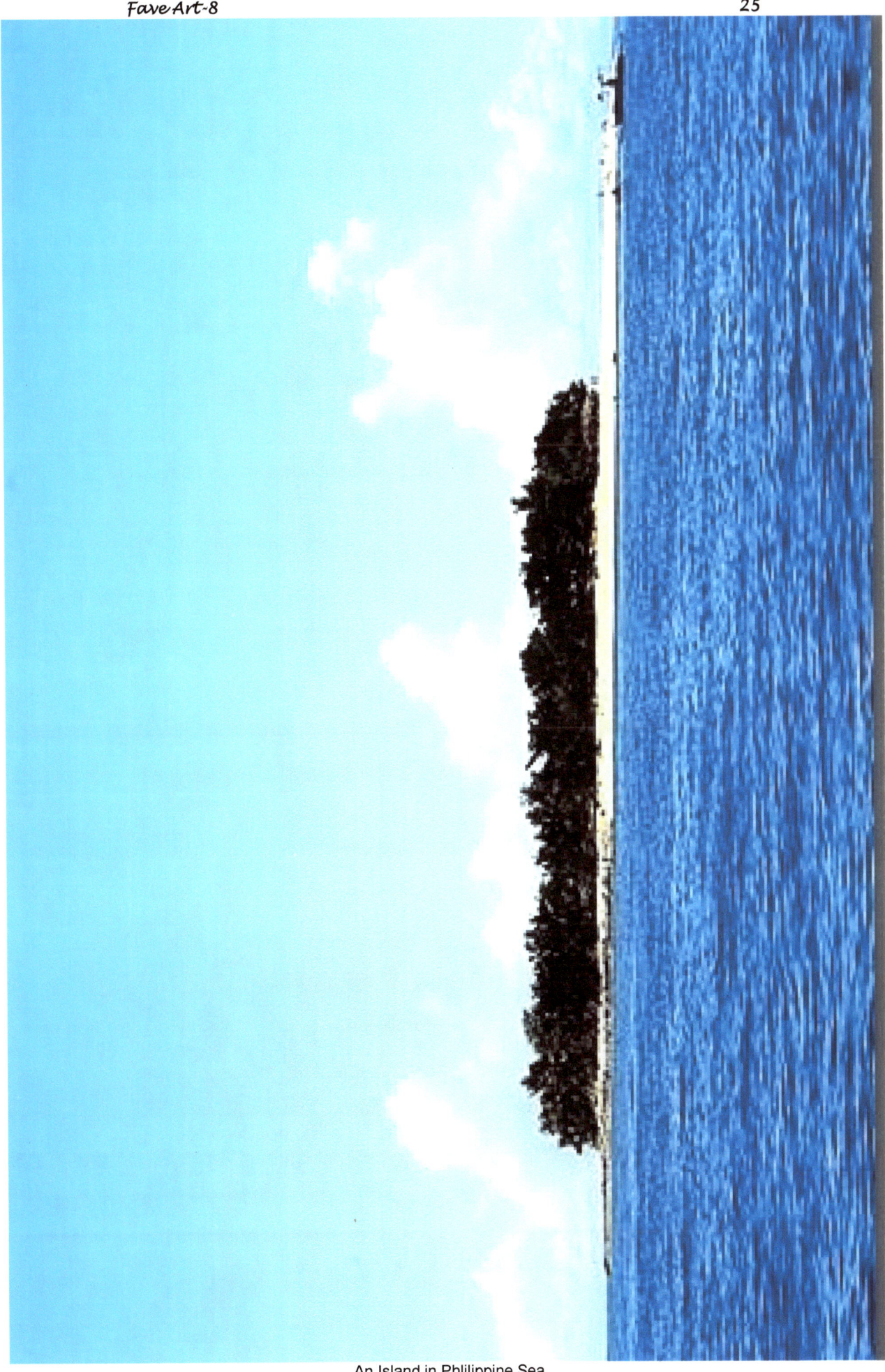

An Island in Phlilippine Sea

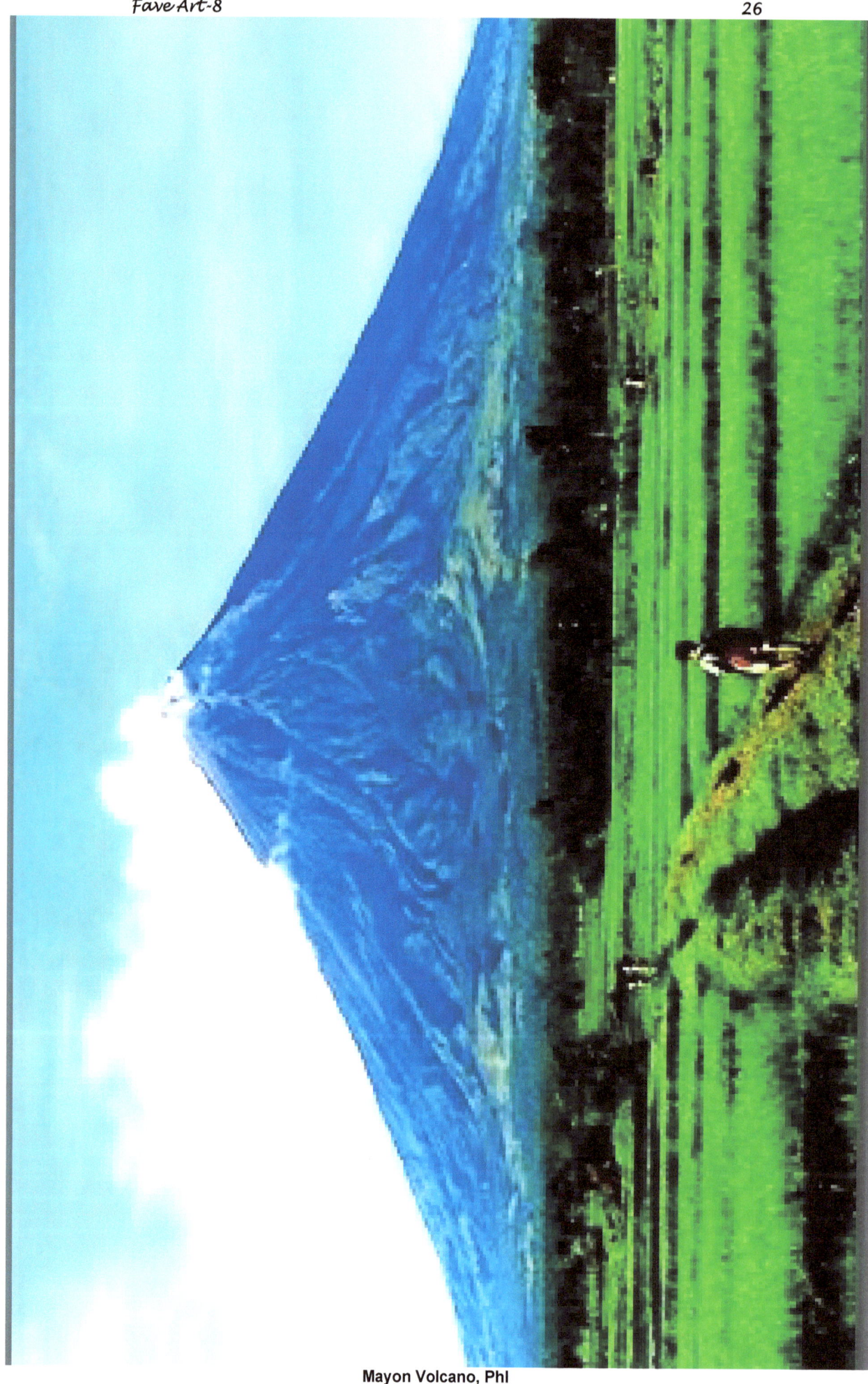

Mayon Volcano, Phl

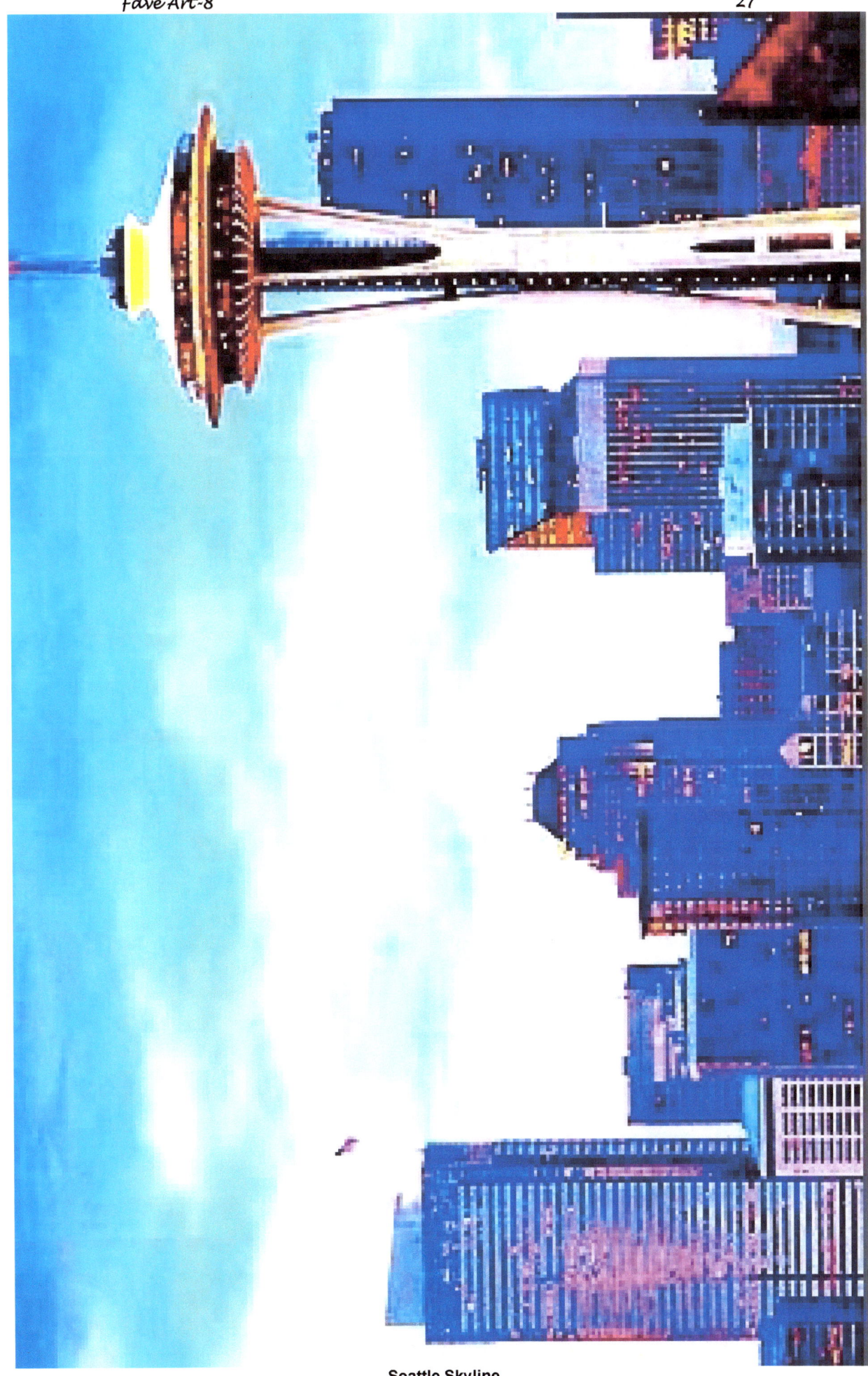

Seattle Skyline

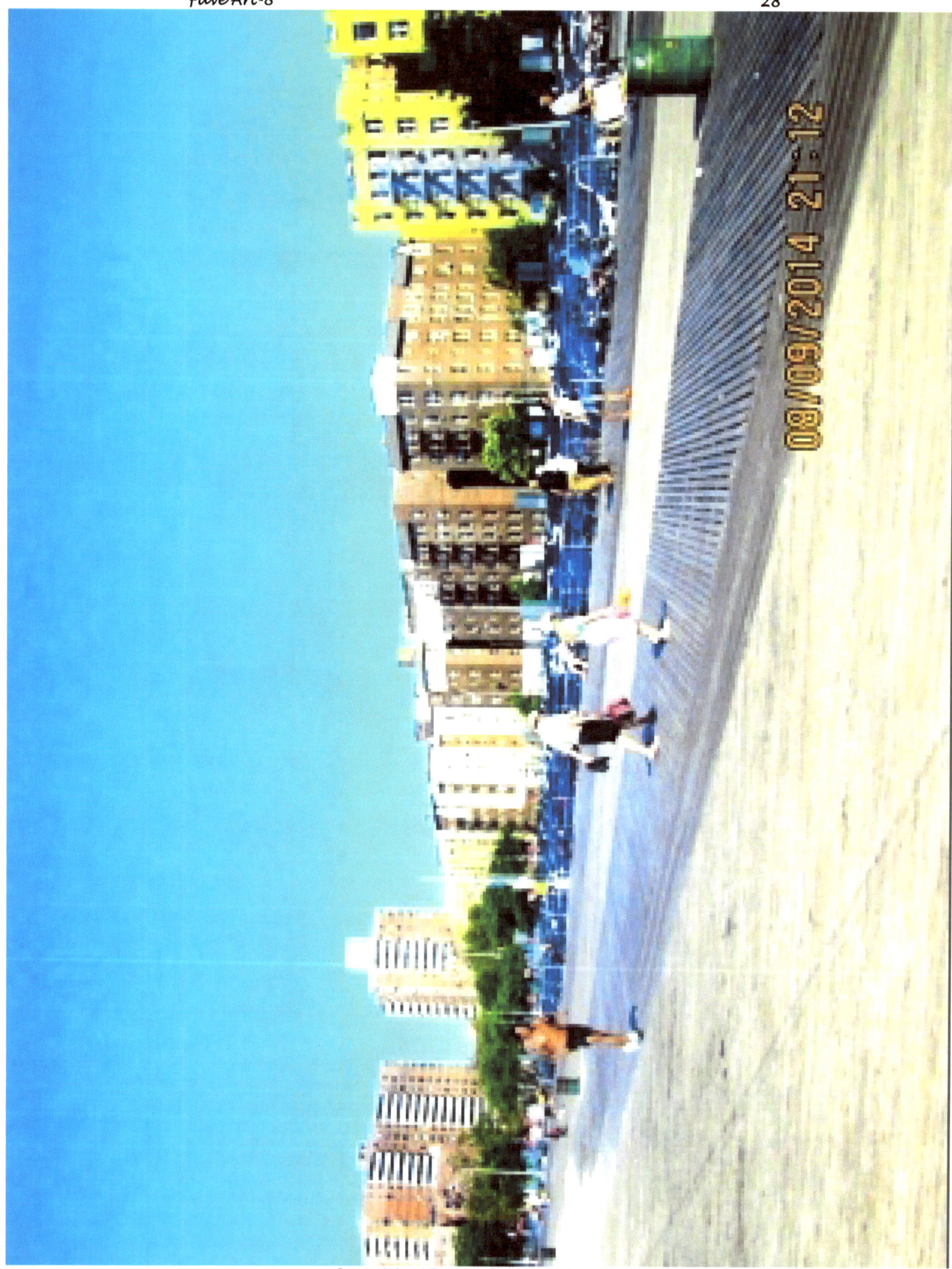

Coney Island Boardwalk in Brooklyn, NY

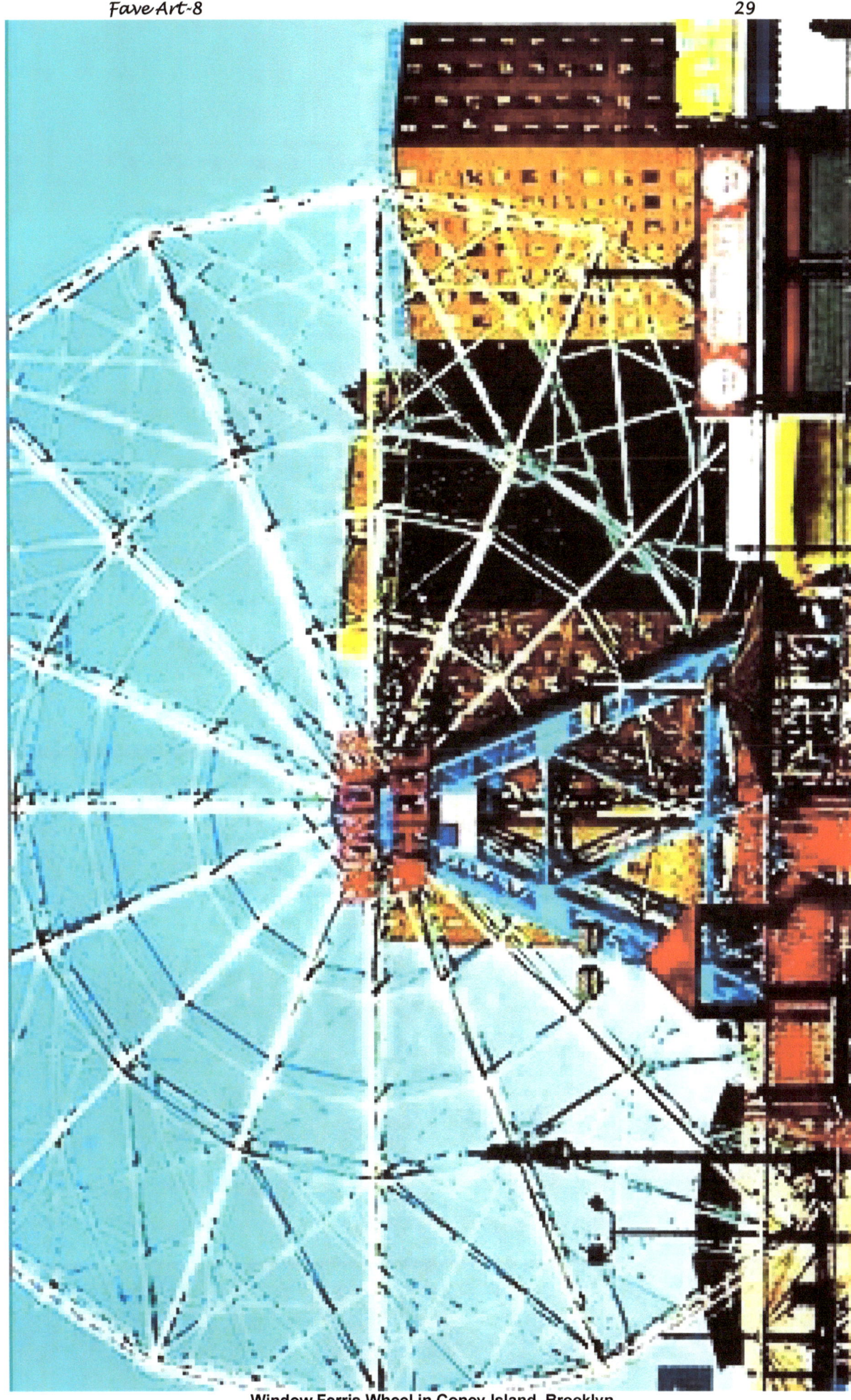

Window Ferris Wheel in Coney Island, Brooklyn

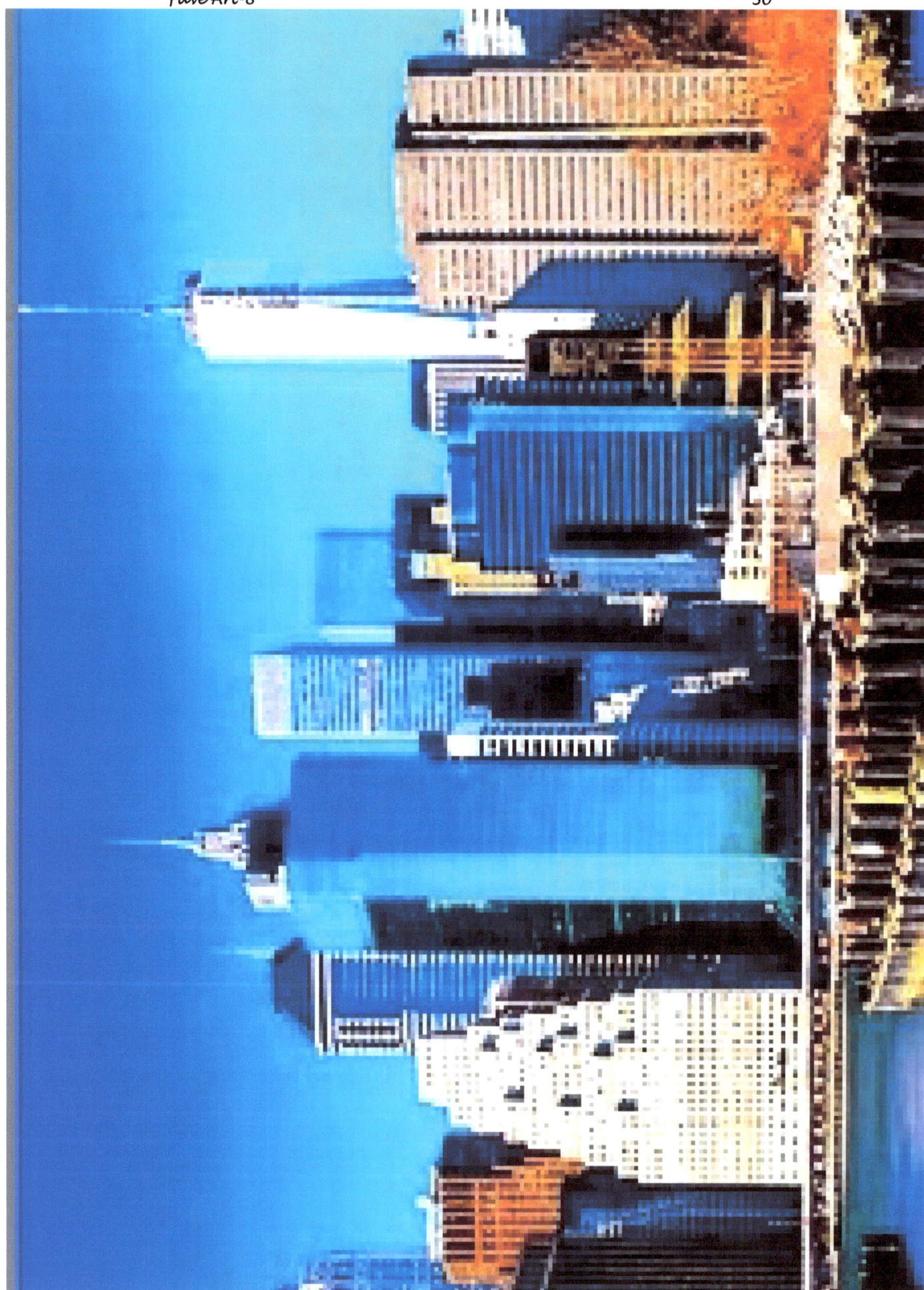

My Manhattan View from Brooklyn

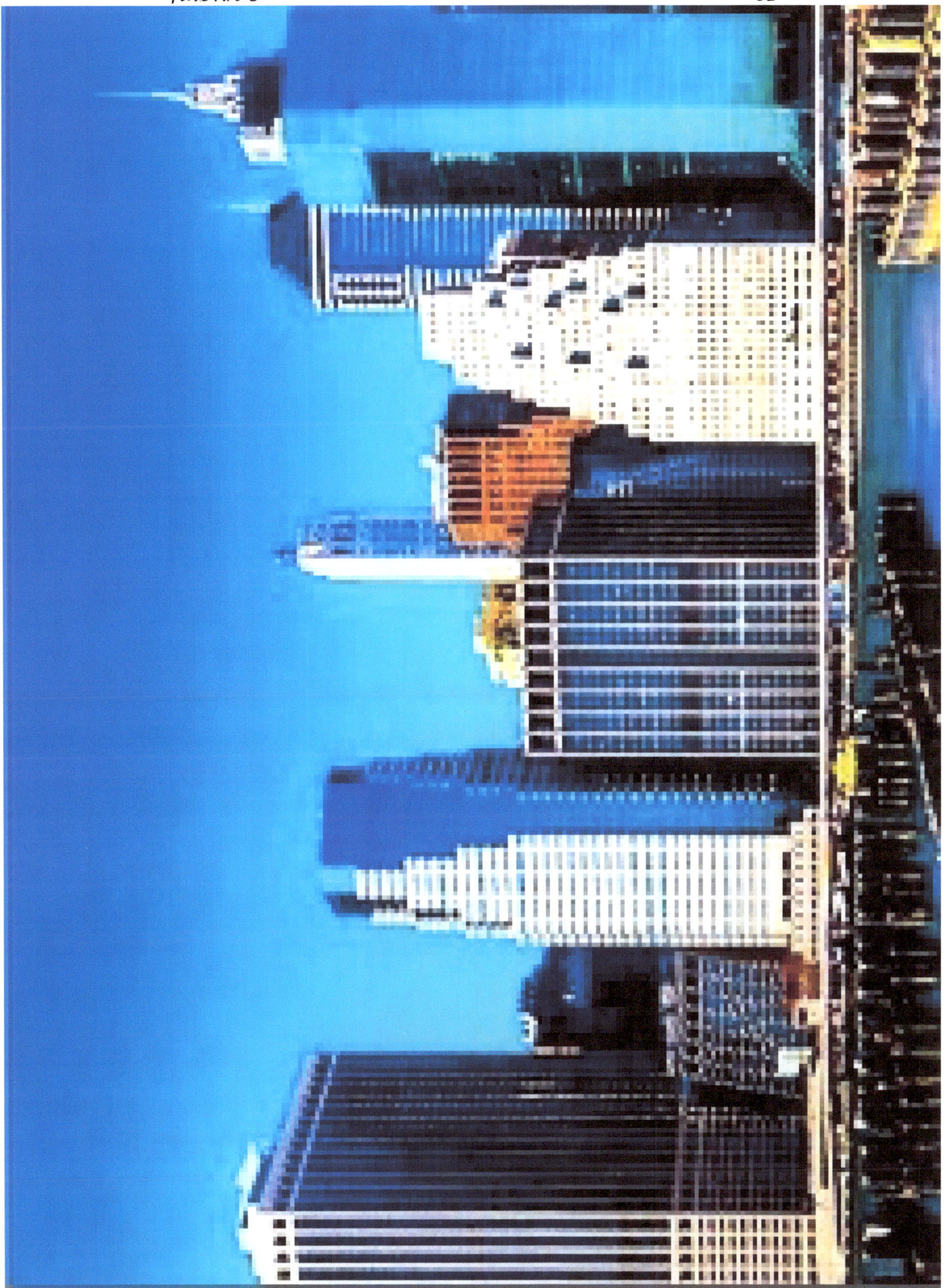

Another view of Manhattan from Brooklyn Side

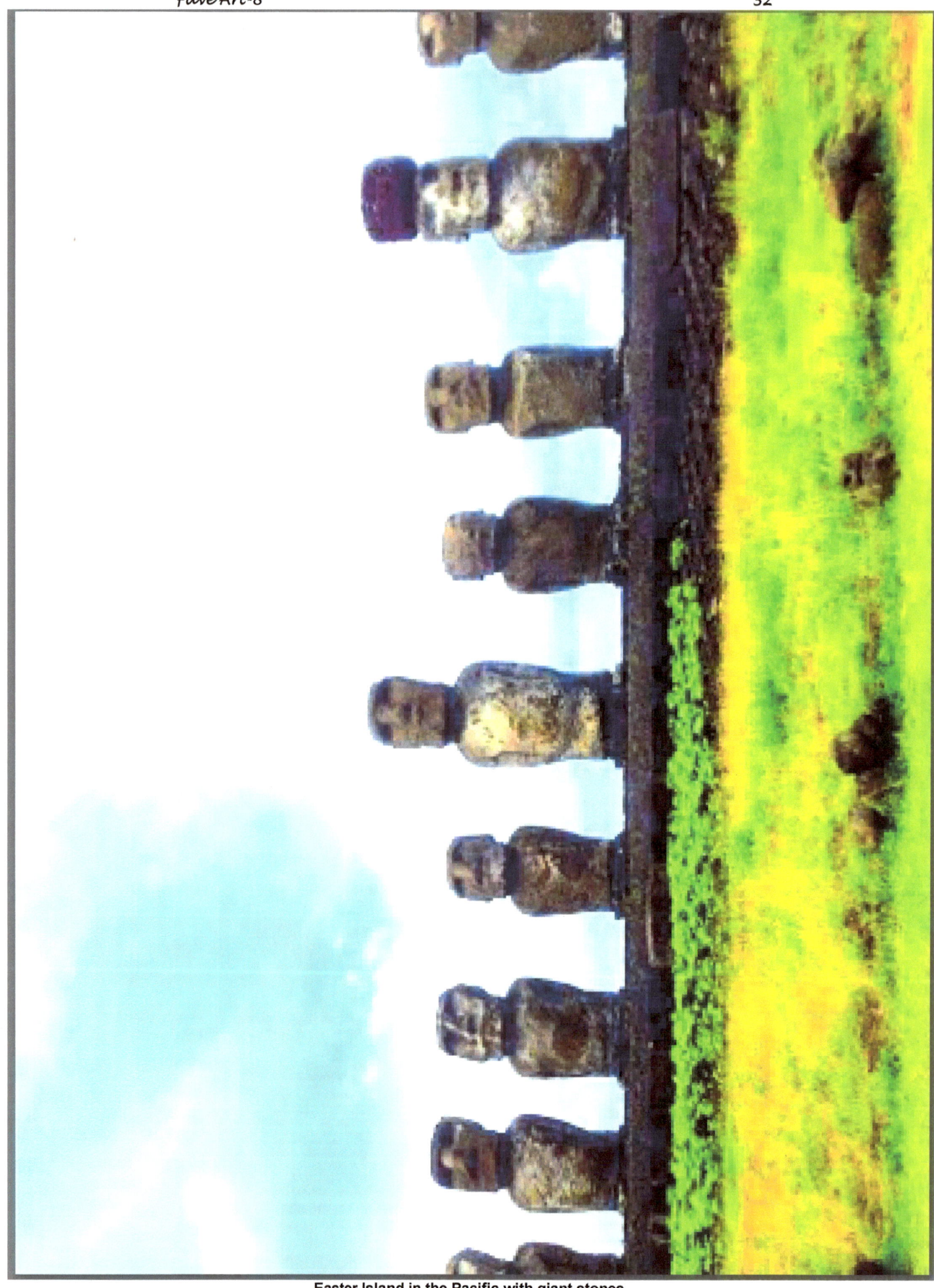

Easter Island in the Pacific with giant stones

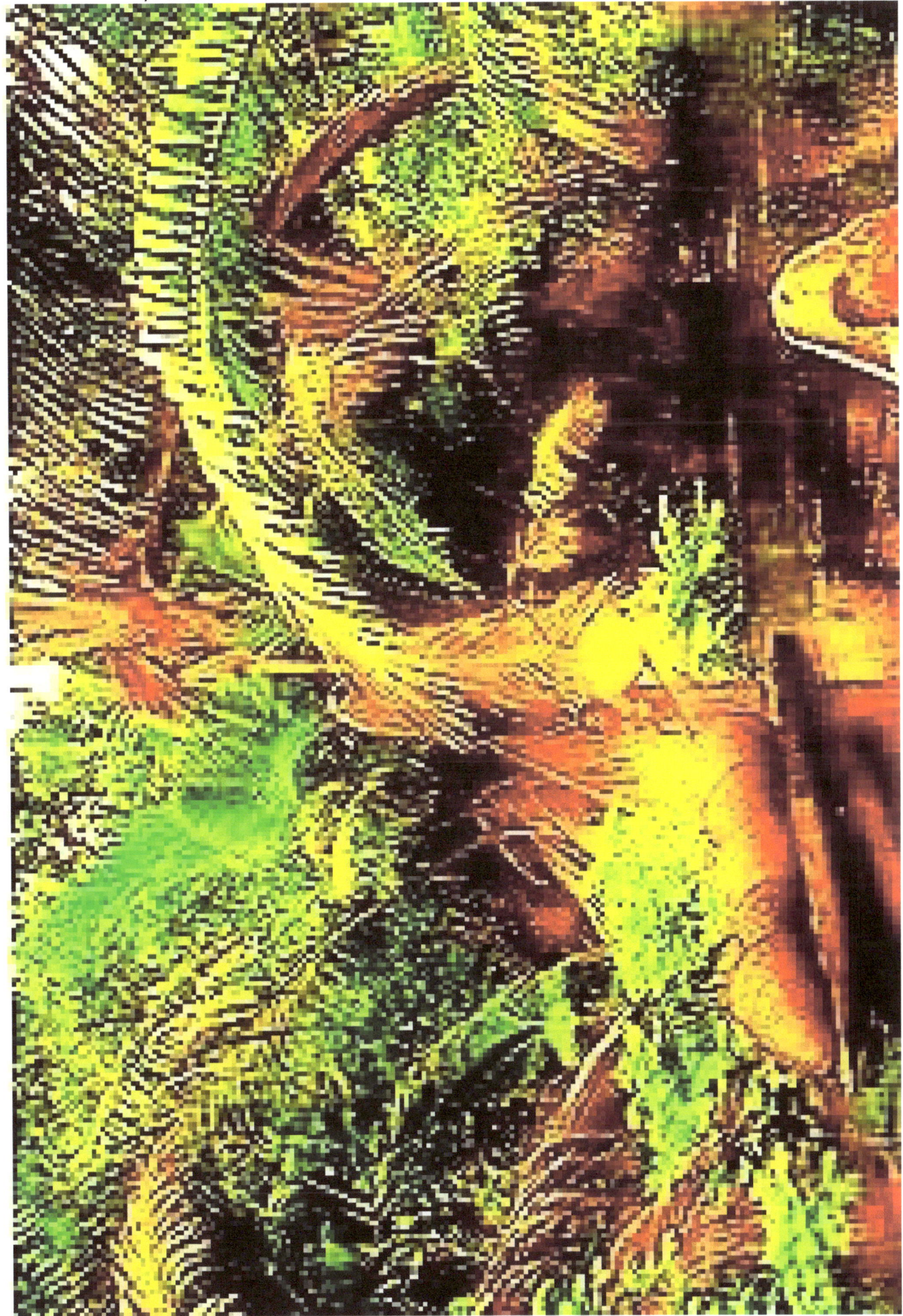

New Guinea Interiors

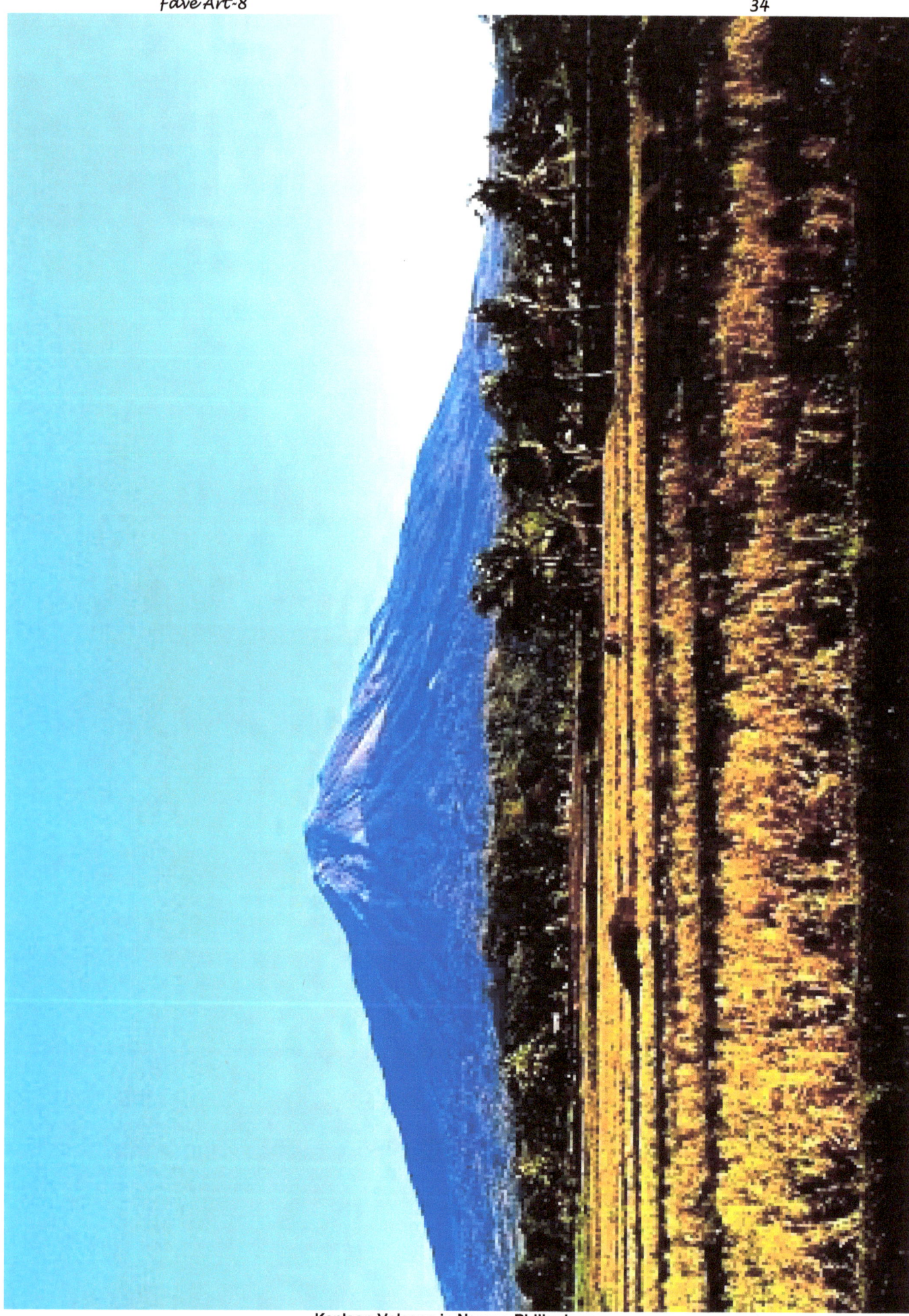

Kanlaon Volcano in Negros Philippines

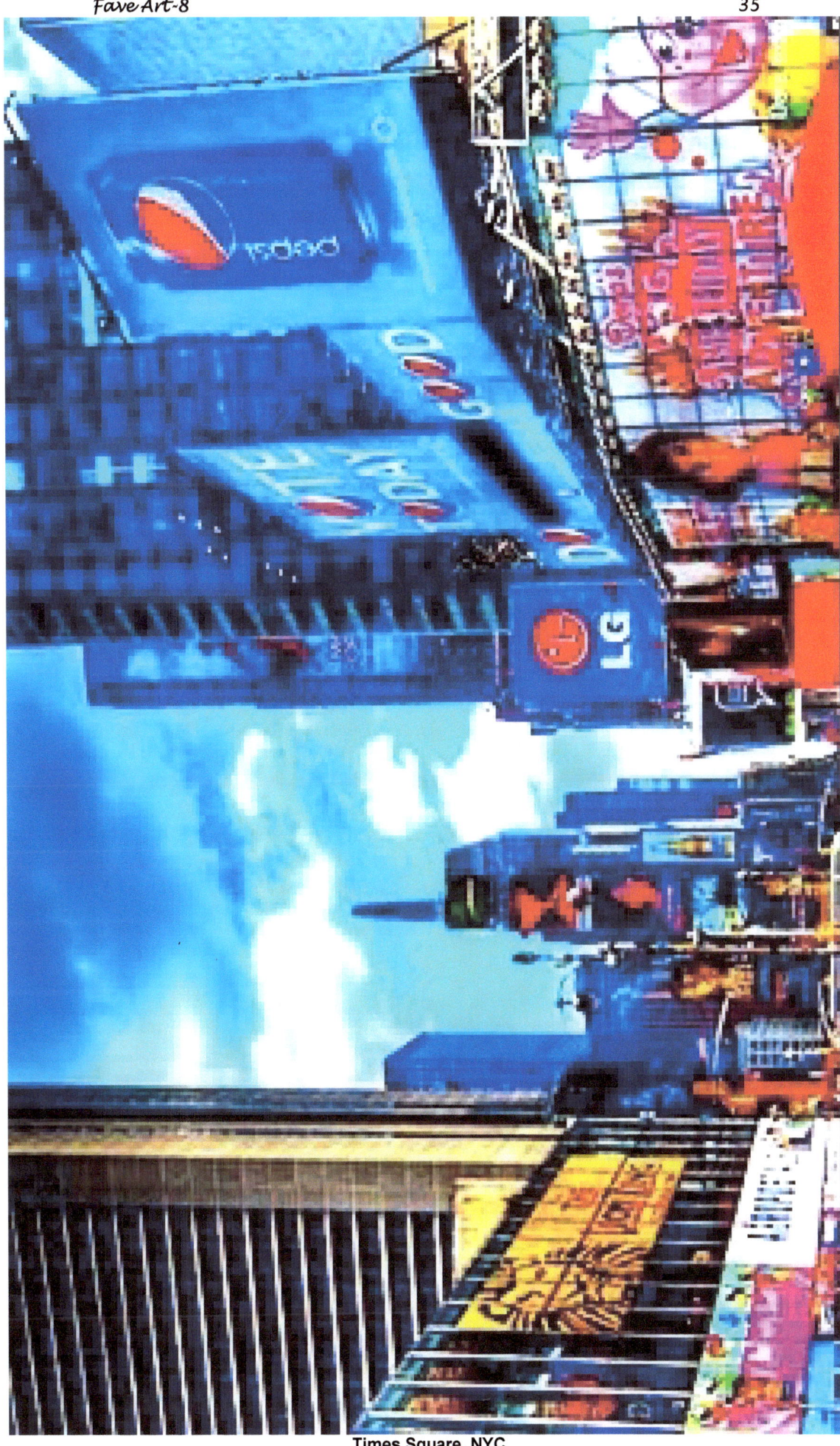

Times Square, NYC

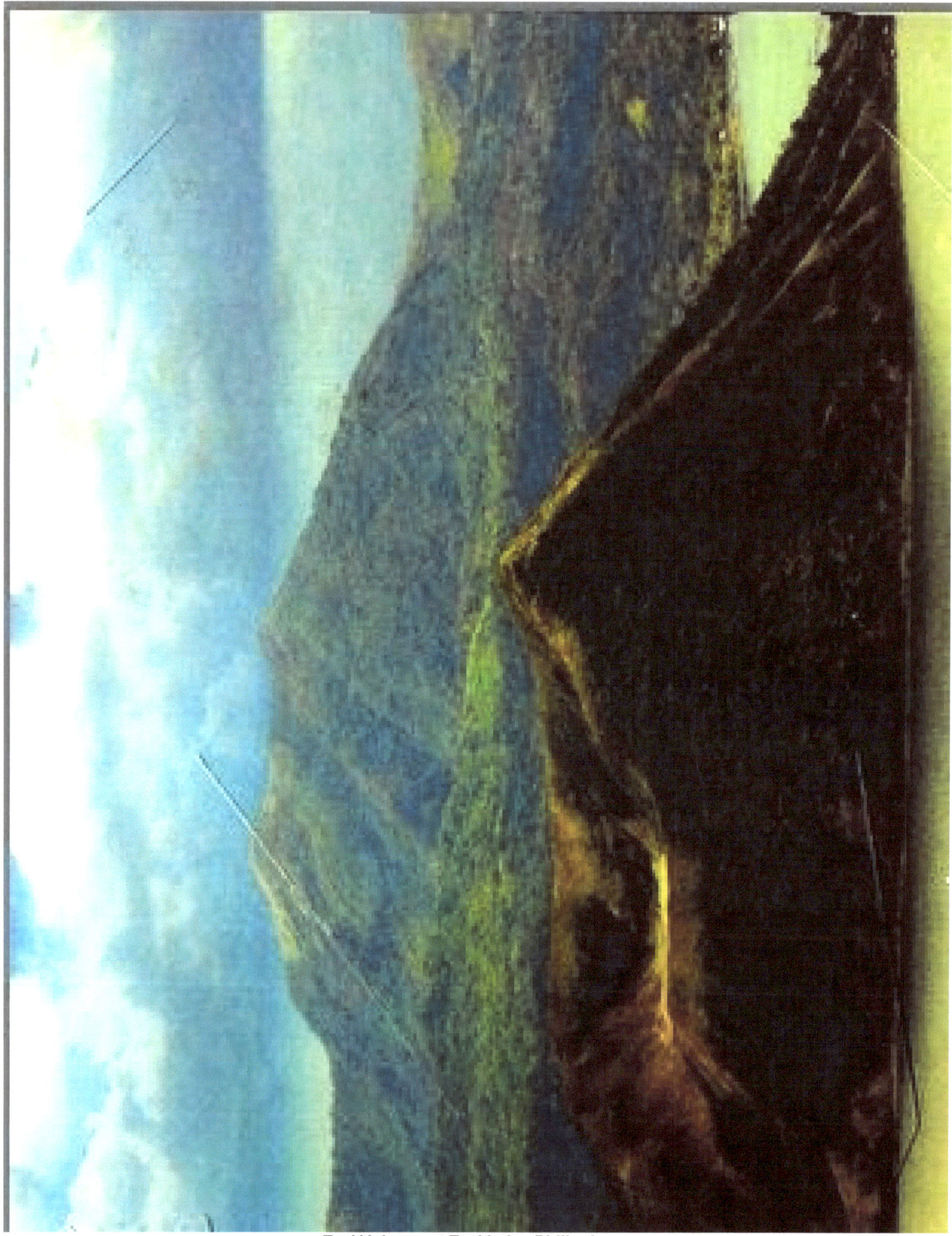

Taal Volcano at Taal Lake, Philippines

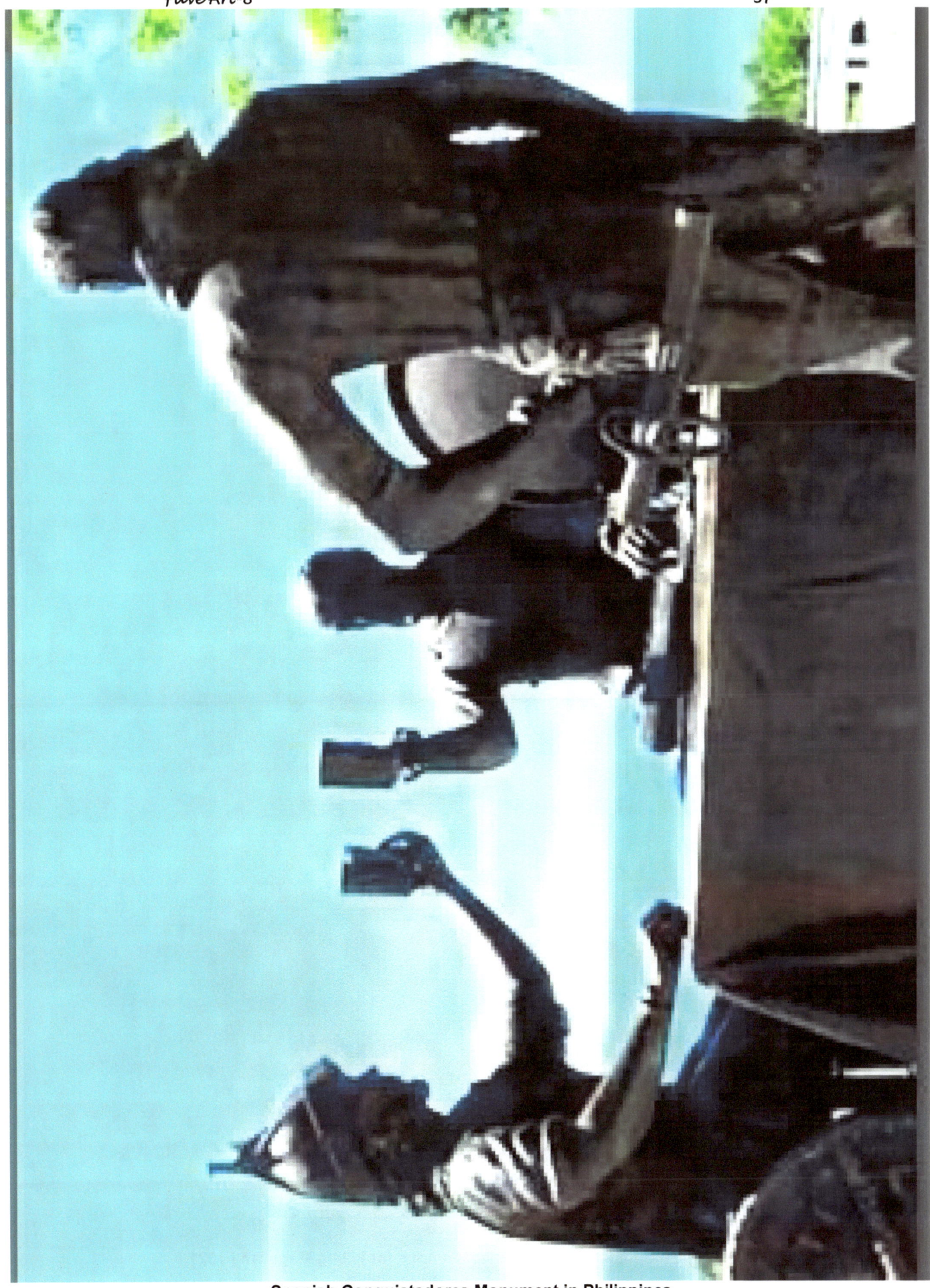

Spanish Conquistadores Monument in Philippines

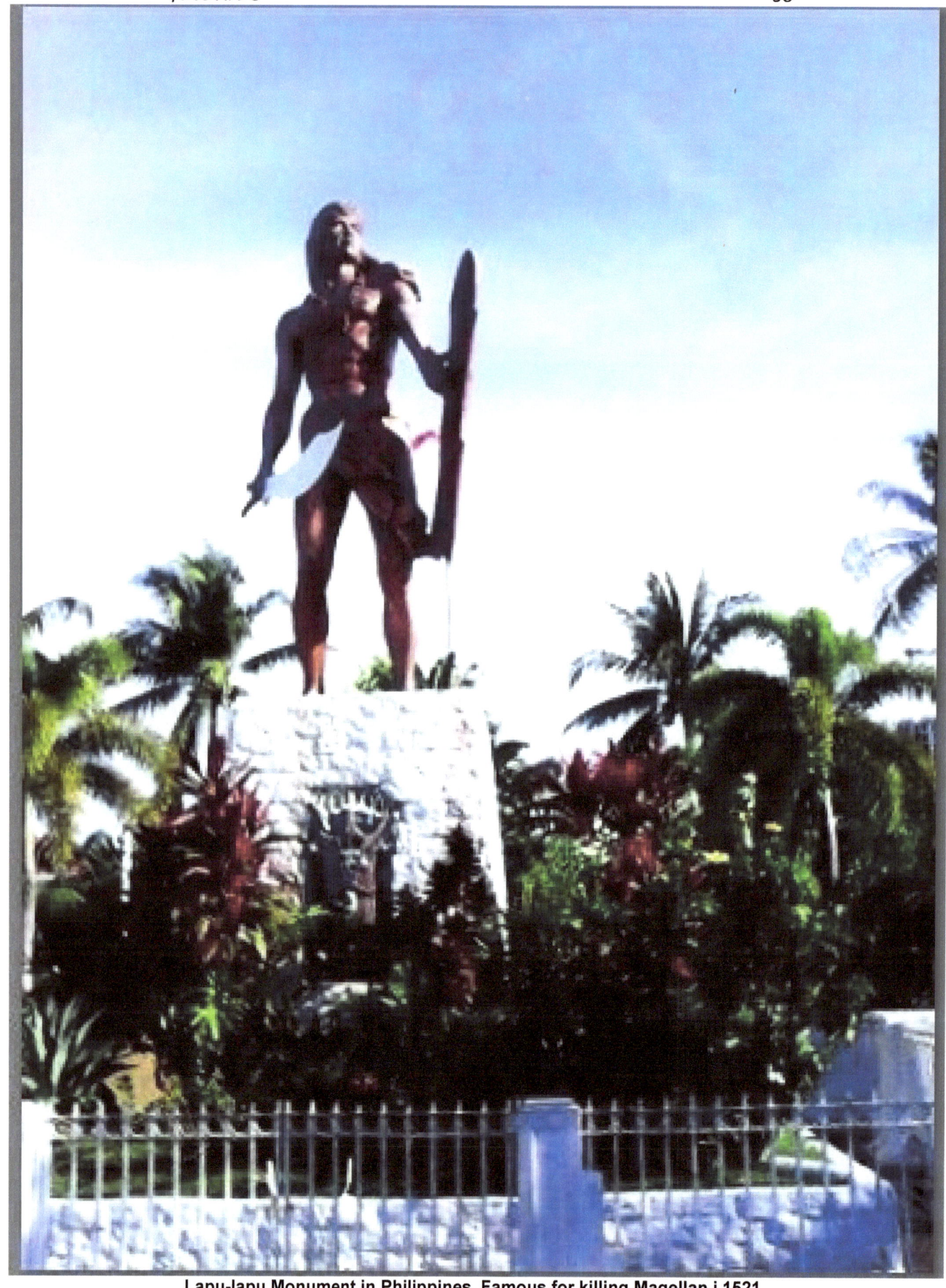

Lapu-lapu Monument in Philippines. Famous for killing Magellan i 1521.

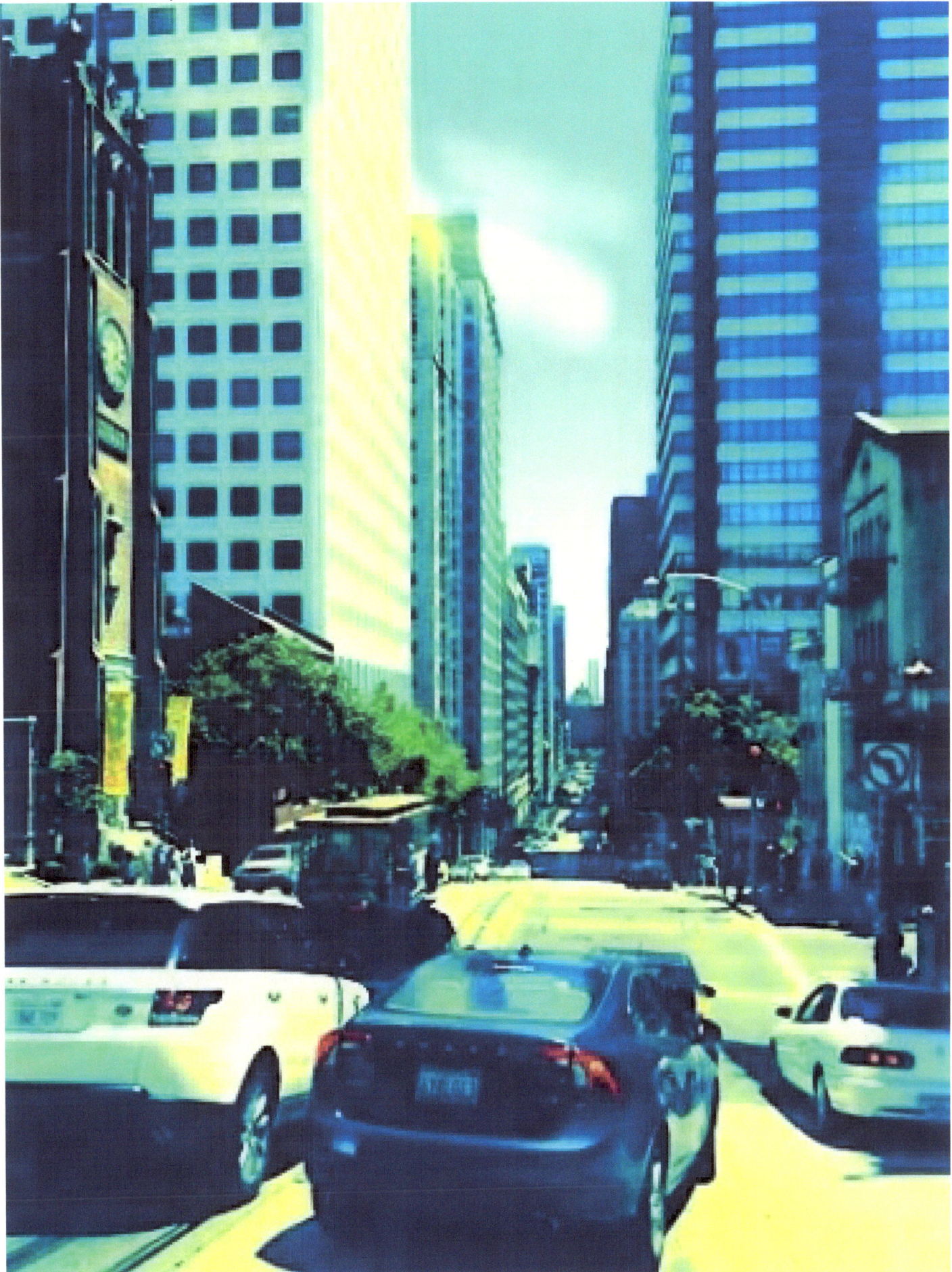

Street of San Francisco, CA, showing cable car and regular traffic.

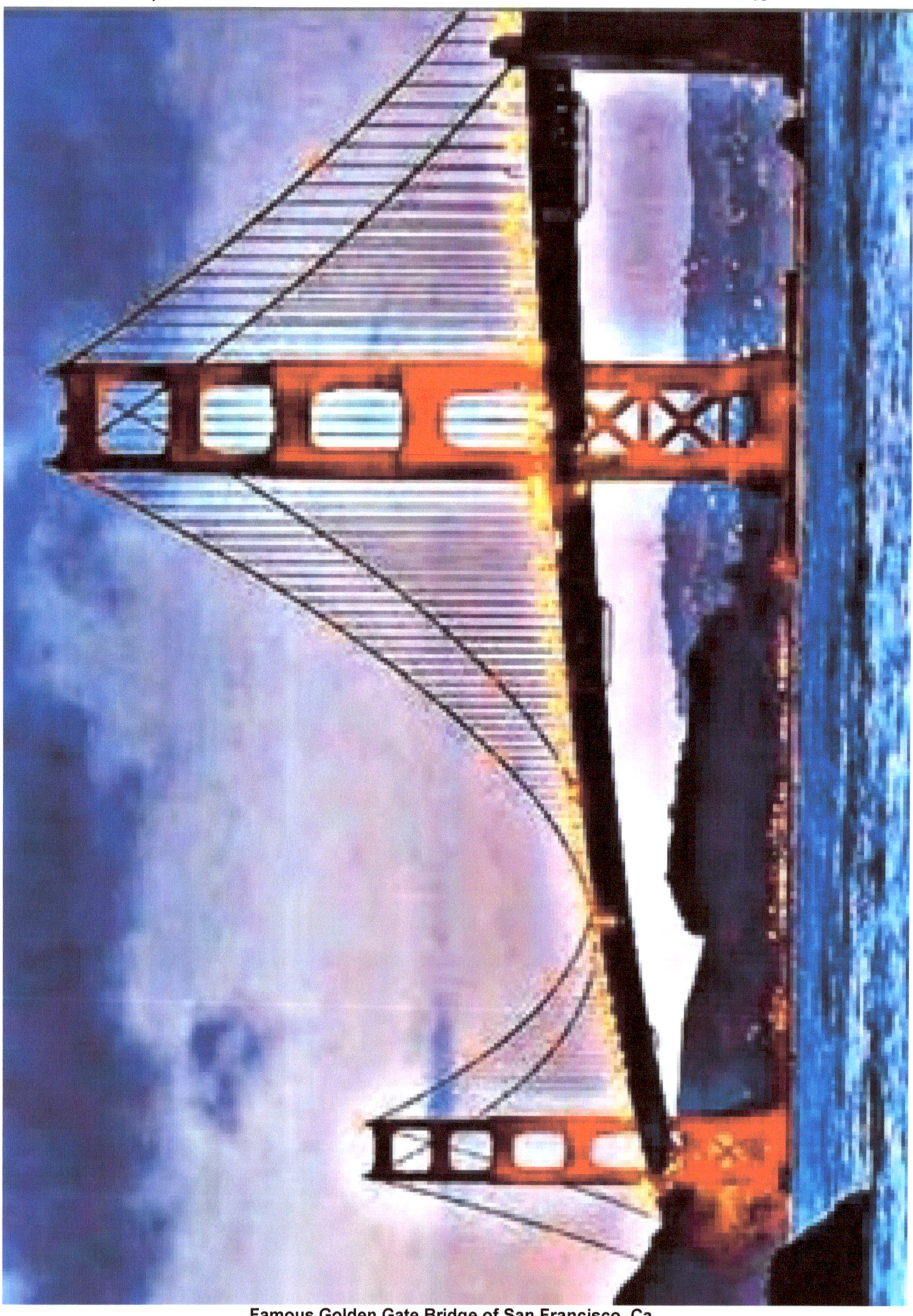

Famous Golden Gate Bridge of San Francisco, Ca.